The Angel of
Dien Bien Phu

An Association of U.S. Army Book

The Angel of Dien Bien Phu

The Sole French Woman at the Decisive Battle in Vietnam

GENEVIÈVE DE GALARD

Translated from the French by Isabelle Surcouf Toms

NAVAL INSTITUTE PRESS
Annapolis, Maryland

Naval Institute Press
291 Wood Road
Annapolis, MD 21402

Library of Congress Cataloging-in-Publication Data
Galard, Geneviève de
  [Femme à Dien Bien Phu. English]
  The angel of Dien Bien Phu : the sole French woman at the decisive battle in Vietnam /
Geneviève de Galard.
      p. cm.
  Includes bibliographical references.
  ISBN 978-1-59114-206-5
  1. Galard, Geneviève de, 1924- 2. Indochinese War, 1946-1954—Personal narratives,
French. 3. Indochinese War, 1946-1954—Medical care. 4. Dien Bien Phu, Battle of,
Điên Biên Phu, Vietnam, 1954. 5. Nurses—France—Biography. 6. France. Armée de
l'air. Groupement des moyens militaires de transport aérien—Biography. 7. Aviation
nursing—France—History—20th century. 8. Aviation nursing—Vietnam—History—20th
century. I. Title.
  DS553.5.G3513 2010
  959.704'142—dc22

                                                                    2010021998

Printed in the United States of America on acid-free paper.

14 13 12 11 10   9 8 7 6 5 4 3 2
First printing

To my husband and my children
To the combatants of Dien Bien Phu of all services
To the youth of France and America,
and all freedom-loving youth of the world

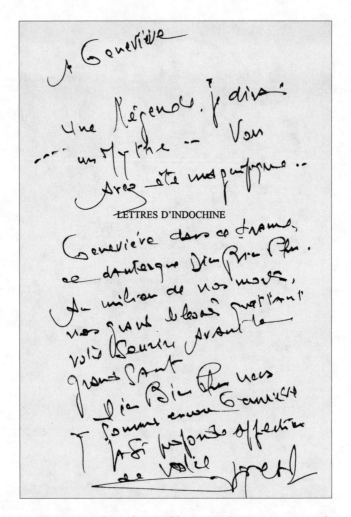

LETTRES D'INDOCHINE

To Geneviève, a legend, I would say a Myth. You were magnificent, Geneviève, in that Dantesque drama of Dien Bien Phu,
in the midst of our dead, our gravely wounded watching you
smile before their grand leap. DBP—we are still there, Geneviève. With profound affection, your Bigeard.

Heroism lies less in the nature of actions than in the manner
in which they are accomplished.

—*Jacques d'Arnoux, The Seven Pillars of Heroism*

Contents

Author's Note

To my American friends:

I have written this book not as a historian, yet with a strong sense of veracity, so that our younger generations may learn some simple truths of which they are never informed but that I must place in history.

The time of which I write was during the Cold War. The French were no longer "colonizing"; they were fellow combatants with the Vietnamese, who were suffering an atrocious civil war in which Communist ideological propaganda was supported by a relentless use of terror. With their participation, France was able to sustain for several years a war that it could not really afford. And we could not have sustained that effort had we not received financial and logistical support from the United States, which helped form the new army of South Vietnam.

As I began work on this book, I remembered the immense effort by the United States in World War II, how it brought victory to the Western world in 1945, and how heavy its losses were in the Pacific. And I recalled the battles France and the United States shared in Korea during the Cold War and the pain suffered by the American people during the last years of the Vietnam War.

What the French gave in Dien Bien Phu also has earned a place in the history of our two countries. Its place in our memories is a witness, even unto sacrificing one's life, to the values that we have shared throughout both our histories: the worth of the individual, a sense of liberty and honor, and the value of giving oneself in a strong patriotism always open to the needs of the world—in fact, a Christian sense of human values that is the basis for the spirit of solidarity that was so strong in the combatants of Dien Bien Phu.

I also remembered the emotions around the world stirred by the heroism of our men and, particularly, the exceptional welcome given me by the United States in their honor.

The title of this book comes from the name that you, Americans, gave me: The Angel of Dien Bien Phu. I present the book to you in heartfelt gratitude and with the strong hope that it will inspire the young people of America.

—*Geneviève de Galard*
Paris, 2010

Foreword

There have been numerous articles, books, and movies about the contributions of men during conflict. However, the contributions of women are often overlooked. Unfortunately, often their colleagues and fellow citizens cannot even imagine their participation during essential moments in history. This propensity, whether intentional or not, is a disservice to those women and to younger women who seek mentors and role models.

For many years I sought information about women military leaders, both to sustain me and to educate other women about their important contributions. However, the response from these women is similar to men singled out for recognition—"I was just doing my job." Personally, I believe it is essential that team members, at every level, understand how their contributions make a difference in the big picture. I am delighted that one of these incredible heroes decided to share her story with the rest of us.

Women have always been volunteers. They have never been drafted, in the United States or abroad. They suffer the same as the men suffer. They have the nightmares and struggles with post-traumatic stress, the guilt of survival, the worries of "Was I good enough? Did I live up to the expectations of my comrades?" In France as in the United States, their fellow citizens have disparaged female service members. People need to tell their stories to educate the citizenry about why people serve their nations.

Geneviève de Galard, a well-educated woman with two baccalaureate degrees, felt a call to duty, a life dedicated to "giving to others," and answered that call. The events that would unfold during her service, being trapped in an enemy's siege and then a prisoner of war, were ones she never imagined. In her story, she describes the multitude of emotions and opportunities she enjoyed while displaying the optimistic and cheerful attitude the men would come to adore in her.

In Vietnam, French paratroopers jumped into battle knowing that their only way out if injured was if an aircraft could land and pick them up. Geneviève de Galard was one of the flight nurses who braved those difficult trips to retrieve the injured soldiers. Not only were the landing strips challenging because of terrain, but the difficulty was heightened due to the intensity of conflict.

I believe that Geneviève de Galard's story is especially important in light of the current struggles around the world with terrorism. She addresses the power of propaganda and its influence on the French citizens who then shunned their involvement with Vietnam, a country subjected to a relentless use of terror on its citizens. A guerrilla war, "a war without mercy," is how she describes the psychological warfare by an adversary that relishes breaking the enemy's morale.

Additionally, her clarity in describing the circumstances, the hopes, and fears of the health-care team and the patients are easily read and riveting—one can see their surroundings and ride the emotional roller-coaster during their defense and imprisonment. Her story demonstrates and resonates with our Army values—loyalty, duty, respect, selfless service, honor, integrity, and personal courage. Finally, the full story of the "Angel of Dien Bien Phu" is told, another gift by this devoted and talented nurse.

In America in 1954 our media coined the phrase "The Angel of Dien Bien Phu" as the way to describe the extraordinary efforts of Genevieve de Galard. After years of silence, she decided that her story was important to share. I believe that you will find this book well worth your time. I hope you share in our gratitude for her nursing care to the frightened and wounded and her contribution to a more a complete history of women in service to their countries.

—*Maj. Gen. Gale S. Pollock* (Ret.), CRNA, FACHE, FAAN

Preface

For a long time I said nothing. I did not wish to feed the publicity of which I had been the object in 1954 after Dien Bien Phu (DBP). I had felt it to be exaggerated and sometimes inappropriate when my comrades, taken prisoner, still suffered in the camps.

In 1954, when I returned to Paris after six weeks at the side of the combatants and the wounded in DBP, then seventeen days at the hands of the Vietminh, I received a letter signed by six paratroopers of the 11th Choc (a French shock parachute regiment) whom I did not know. One of them was Hélie de Saint Marc, who had not yet attained the fame he has today. They wrote, "Set aside all propaganda and publicity. Our comrades do not need articles or movies. History will judge them. You were with them, that is sufficient." I agreed totally with this letter and I kept silent.

This reticence has been my rule in life. I did, however, express myself now and then, when the judgments passed on the combatants in Indochina seemed to me too partial or too unfair. Then I would speak up or write.

I also occasionally accepted invitations to speak before reserve officers or close relatives or friends, and I never refused to address young people. But these occasions were very limited because my responsibilities as ward counselor in the 17th Arrondissement kept me very involved for eighteen years and because it has always been difficult and even painful for me to evoke those memories.

But in the darkness, time was doing its work. Three years ago, Hélie de Saint Marc, returning to his letter of 1954, incited me to write: "More than ever before, I believe in the power of testimonies." Silent for many years, he had broken the silence.

My municipal job was over and I started reflecting on his advice. Then I remembered the passionate interest of the teen-aged girls before whom I had been asked to speak of DBP. I remembered also the look in the eyes of the children who had attended the ceremony of the flame at the Arc de Triomphe, one day in November, when I had evoked for them the courage of the combatants at DBP.

With the peace that comes with distance in time, when nothing, neither vanity nor lies, can muddy the memory, there remains the raw experience, naked, terrible, and great at the same time. That is what must be passed on to the next generations.

A woman twenty years my junior, Béatrice Bazil, helped me organize the dozens of pages of my writing. I owe her much; one does not improvise oneself into an author. Our collaboration was an exchange. I opened her eyes to those difficult years. She was only five years old when the battle for DBP was taking place. It created true bonds of friendship between us.

During those weeks and months, I was reabsorbed in those painful memories; they awakened me at night. I heartily thank those who, through their own remembrances, helped recapture my own, and those who guided me on this uncertain path.

From here on, history may speak.

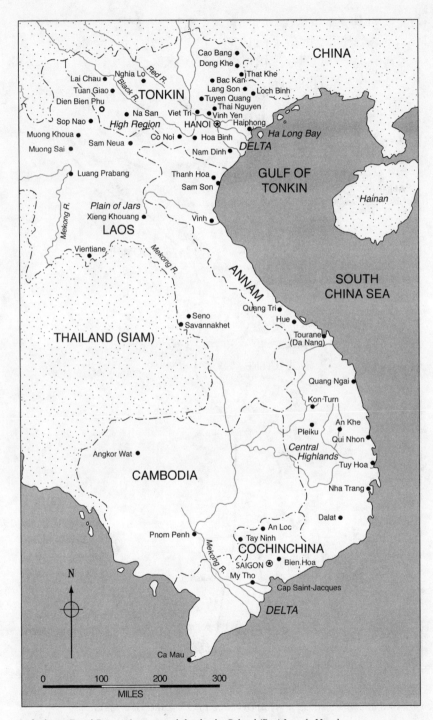

Indochina. *David Rennie, from original sketches by Colonel (Ret.) Jean de Heaulme*

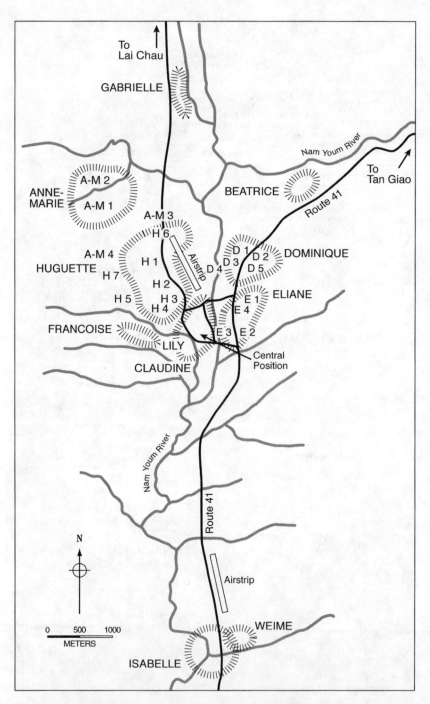

Dien Bien Phu. *David Rennie, from original sketches by Colonel (Ret.) Jean de Heaulme*

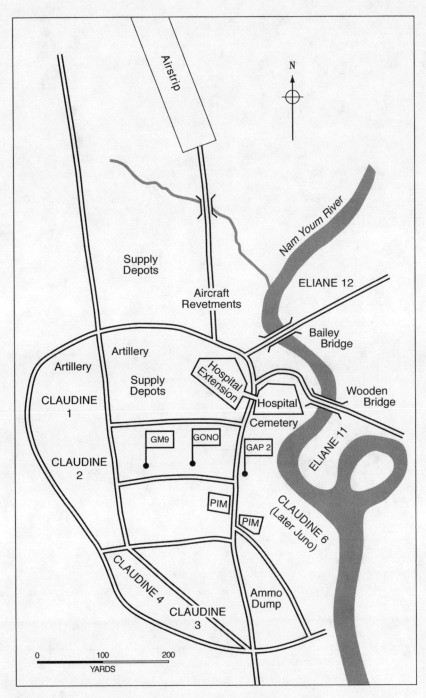

The central position at Dien Bien Phu. *David Rennie, from original sketches by Colonel (Ret.) Jean de Heaulme*

The Angel of
Dien Bien Phu

INTRODUCTION
Toward Dien Bien Phu: The Historical Context

Circumstances that led to Geneviève de Galard being the only French woman caught in the maelstrom of Dien Bien Phu were long in the brewing.

French colonialism in Indochina rose from the compulsion to spread Catholicism and Western ways (*la mission civilisatrice*) and from the race to keep up with the British and Dutch in economically exploiting Southeast Asia. By the first half of the nineteenth century the politicians, businessmen, and financiers of London, Paris, and Amsterdam were vying with one another over the riches that surely would flow from colonies of the Orient. Few, if any, could foresee the ultimate costs of those early fortunes gained and lost in terms of national treasure later wasted and blood spilled.

The brutal reprisals of Vietnamese rulers against early European Catholic missionaries and their Vietnamese converts gave France reason for outright colonization. In 1858 the French annexed three provinces around Saigon; in 1867 they annexed three more in an effort to quell the bands of guerrillas who were making life intolerable for the French colonialists, and by 1873 all of Indochina was under French control—Laos and Cambodia to the west, and Vietnam, which included Tonkin in the North, Annam in the middle, and Cochinchina in the South.

On the positive side the "civilizing mission" of the French showed itself in security, education, jurisprudence systems, and many civic improvements: roads, railroads, docks, canals, hospitals, schools—engineering projects of all kinds—and in the many types of employment that developed. Critics could argue that all were for the benefit of the French, but in fact a large segment of the Vietnamese people began to live a lifestyle more like that of the progressive nations of the West, and they readily saw its advantages. Many, perhaps most, Vietnamese were caught in a contradictory relationship with the French, admiring and emulating their Western culture yet resenting their domination.

The earliest French military forces were naval with their usual component of naval infantry on board for shore action. Later small ground units were introduced and based ashore as the need arose. Supplementing the white French forces were the *Jaunes* (Yellows), Indochinese troops who since 1859 had served the French.

When World War II broke out on September 1, 1939, with the German invasion of Poland, French Indochina was in a pitifully weak condition. At that time in Indochina, with an estimated population of 30 million, there were fewer than 40,000 French residents and only 49,100 troops of all kinds in the military forces, including the auxiliaries, 35,400 of whom were Indochinese. Twenty-two thousand Europeans were in the civil service, that is to say, comparatively few. European businessmen were dispersed in large villages and cities, and European settlers of the land dotted a vast countryside.

Cut off from their support base half a world away, ill equipped and sparsely supplied, the French were faced with the prospect of defending against the enormously powerful Japanese, who had overrun coastland China and were set on conquering all of Asia. France itself was soon to be invaded by the Germans, Britain was trying to defend its isles, and the United States was determined not to commit forces, content to supply its allies with the weapons of war. Sailing out of Vietnamese ports, the French navy had one cruiser and four cutters to defend a 1,500-mile coastline against the mighty Japanese navy. The French air force in Indochina had about one hundred outdated planes, mostly observation and utility or transport aircraft. After the Germans invaded France in June 1940 and the Vichy government of Marshal Pétain was established, the governor general of Indochina, Admiral Jean Decoux, tried to preserve as much as he could from Japanese encroachment but was forced by circumstances to cooperate with them.

In September 1940 the Japanese forced the new Vichy French administration of Indochina to turn over three airfields in Tonkin, followed in July 1941 by eight more in southern Indochina, accompanied by the withdrawal of the French garrisons from those places. On July 28, 1941, four months before the attack on Pearl Harbor, the Japanese marched into Saigon and established their supremacy by occupying key positions throughout Vietnam.

Since the 1941 Japanese occupation, the Vichy French administrative structure of Indochina had been left in control, and their ground and air forces—though feeble—had proven strong enough to battle Siam (Thailand) to a draw in a border war. At the same time the small French navy won a decisive battle over Siam's fleet, significantly improving French morale. But a devastating blow to the French would occur on March 9, 1945. By that time the Japanese in Indochina were in an increasingly precarious position, with advancing American forces in the Pacific placing them in a stranglehold. The possibility of the French forces within Indochina suddenly taking the side of the Allies was real and immediate.

The time had come to act. In Saigon, during the early evening of that day, the Japanese commander secretly issued an ultimatum to turn over administrative control of all Indochina to the Japanese and to disarm and confine French troops to barracks, an order the high commissioner refused. Prepositioned Japanese troops swept down upon startled French garrisons throughout Indochina and quickly subdued most of them. Many, though, managed to retain their arms and fiercely fight back. This was especially true in Tonkin, where, for example, the Lang Son and Dong Dang garrisons put up a fierce defense. General Sabattier and General Alessandri were able to conduct a fighting withdrawal to the Chinese frontier with a significant part of the Tonkin division and attachments. Many French were hideously massacred, and much of the remainder were imprisoned under unspeakably brutal conditions.

As early as 1943 the Free French under General Charles de Gaulle had conceived a plan for the five Indochina states to attain autonomy, but within the planned Associated States of the French Union. De Gaulle believed that to do this in an orderly fashion, French governance had to be reestablished first. The French made plans for a two-division and one-brigade French force to be part of the Allied forces to defeat the Japanese in the Pacific. Quite certainly de Gaulle also had in mind driving the Japanese from Indochina. The first actual element of this French force was a Corps Léger d'Intervention (CLI), a commando group of about 1,800 men. They would parachute into distant bush areas throughout Indochina to harass and attack vital communication centers. Some of this was done, including a group inserted at remote Dien Bien Phu (DBP), but in August 1945 atom bombs were dropped on Japan, catching everyone by surprise.

Throughout the war the Vietnamese Communists under Ho Chi Minh had sometimes fought the French, sometimes the Japanese, sometimes both at the same time. In any event they were inspired by the Japanese humiliation of the French. Asian men had actually conquered Western- ers, so why could not the Vietnamese gain their independence? Ho Chi Minh and his military commander, Vo Nguyen Giap, had patiently and firmly taken control of the Vietnam independence movement by subter- fuge, cruelty, assassinations, kindness, rewards, and promises—whatever would work to achieve their ends.

The political and social elements of the Communists' struggle for power had been firmly wedded to the military component from early times, when Giap formed "armed propaganda teams" in Tonkin. If per- suasion or coercion wouldn't work, the teams would resort to a more severe method—terrorism. Significantly, in August and September 1945, Ho and Giap cemented the Communist role in the independence move- ment by overcoming the Viet Nam Quoc Dan Dang (VNQDD), the old- est of the independence parties (but not Communist), in assassinations and small but fierce battles northwest of Hanoi. The seeds of civil war had been planted.

By exercising a variety of means, the Communists had gained sub- stantial support among the populace, especially in Tonkin. The confused situation caused by the Japanese intention to surrender catapulted Ho into action. In Hanoi on September 2, 1945, the day of formal Japa- nese capitulation aboard the battleship *Missouri*, to the cheers of a huge crowd, Ho Chi Minh proclaimed the founding of the Provisional Gov- ernment of the Democratic Republic of Vietnam (DRV). Murders of Frenchmen and those Vietnamese who continued to oppose the Vietminh now began in earnest. So with World War II barely concluded, the stage was set for a new round of war. If the French were to have any hope of regaining control of Indochina, they had to act, and quickly. Saigon was a powder keg set to explode. All was chaos, with the Communists incit- ing the people to riot.

By Allied agreement South East Asia Command (SEAC), headed by the British, had been given the mission of ensuring order in Indochina south of the sixteenth parallel (which was just south of Da Nang), and dis- arming and repatriating the Japanese. The only French military men from the exterior now in Indochina were the tattered remnants of some small detachments of the CLI commandos, who had been inserted months and weeks earlier. British major general Douglas D. Gracey landed the first units of his 20th Indian Division in Saigon on September 11, followed the next day by a company of French commandos from CLI, now renamed the 5th Colonial Infantry Regiment. With chaos continuing, Gracey rearmed as well as he could the small number of imprisoned French colonial soldiers in Saigon who were in any kind of physical shape to fight after months of horrendous mistreatment, and he declared martial law and took over key buildings and facilities. A Communist leader wrote, "On September 23, armed and protected by the British forces, the French colonialists launched their attack and occupied Saigon. Our people replied by force of arms, and from that moment, our heroic resistance began." The Saigon area exploded in violence, and 150 civilian French men, women, and children were massacred by a Communist-led mob.

On October 5 Lieutenant General Philippe Leclerc, commander of the French Expeditionary Force on its way to Saigon, flew into Tan Son Nhut and a few days later told a hysterically joyful French crowd he had come to reclaim France's inheritance. He also told them to be patient and to respect the Vietnamese people, who would have a place in the new French Union.

Soon the arrival of more French units allowed Gracey to push outward from Saigon. Part of this effort was the first major French operation under Leclerc, a combined land and waterways thrust into the Mekong Delta south of Saigon by a reconstituted element of Leclerc's former World War II 2nd Armored Division outfitted with surplus American and British equipment, everything from boots, headgear, and rifles to jeeps, half-tracks, and tanks. They were all volunteers, and this became the case throughout the war when French law prohibited conscripts from being sent to Indochina. The 2nd Armored unit included some women: the famous, incredibly courageous Rochambelles ambulance nurse unit. When the task force had embarked at Marseilles, an area of great strength of the French Communist Party, crowds had thrown rocks and tomatoes at their rail and truck transports to the docks.

Beginning in Cochinchina around Saigon and spreading in all directions, a ferocious guerrilla war—*une guerre sans merci,* "a war without mercy"—soon was being fought. The Vietminh waged anticolonial war against the French and a civil war against those of their countrymen who resisted them. In metropolitan France a strong anticolonial, antiwar feeling would grow until it infected much of the electorate, and French politics would operate in this hostile atmosphere throughout the long years of the Indochina War.

Toward the end of 1945 Leclerc told the new high commissioner and the French government that a lasting military solution was impossible and that serious planning should proceed toward a negotiated settlement. He tried, through the commissioner, to effect a cease-fire and establish a compromise Vietnamese government, an effort that ultimately failed. Meanwhile, the war went on. Despite constant ambushes and sabotage throughout much of Cochinchina and southern Annam, by the spring of 1946 French forces had opened main supply routes during the day (the night belonged to the Vietminh). Now it was time for Leclerc to turn his attention to Tonkin in the North, where Ho's DRV was claiming legitimacy as the sole government of Vietnam. Culling forces from those in the South and adding to them newly arrived units, Leclerc moved elements by sea to the Haiphong area. There they were confronted by the Chinese, who had come to repatriate Japanese troops in Vietnam north of Da Nang. After initial sharp clashes with Chinese units a cease-fire was achieved, and hopes were high for a peaceful resolution of the Vietnamese problem.

Elections throughout Vietnam resulted in a shaky Democratic Republic with Ho as its president. A summer conference at Fontainebleau, France, ended in failure to achieve an accord on Vietnam's status within a French Union; however, a modus vivendi was agreed upon by the two parties that could have brought some stability had the terms been honored by both sides. Unfortunately, such was not the case, and on December 19, 1946, massive insurrection broke out in Hanoi. From this time forward the pattern of the war became one of continuing guerrilla warfare in Cochinchina and southern Annam, plus ferocious battles against regional and main-force units in northern Annam, parts of Laos, and throughout Tonkin.

Just as Saigon and the area surrounding it was key to control in the South, Hanoi was key in the North. Two French military commands in Vietnam were established, each headed by a major general (three stars in the French army). Over them was the commander in chief, a lieutenant general (four stars), and, in one instance, a general of the army (five stars). And over him, responsible for all five Indochina states, was the high commissioner or governor general. On a few occasions the commissioner and commander in chief were one and the same person.

From that first French action in the Mekong Delta, the French were to discover they were pitted against not only a wily foe but also the terrain, weather, and climate. The head of the fledgling navy in Indochina had warned Leclerc that "Cochinchina was no Sahara"—the Sahara being where Leclerc had been an armor commander on hard-packed ground, allowing him broad sweeping moves. And Leclerc had soon discovered the truth of that warning when his tanks were held up by the enemy breaching the road and they were not able to get off it and maneuver in the rice paddies and swamps alongside.

The terrain and climate of Tonkin and northern Annam would prove to be just as difficult. The fertile Red River Delta around Hanoi and Haiphong, with its many rice paddies, canals, and rivers, would present huge challenges to French units equipped and trained to fight a European-style war. And to the west of Hanoi toward northern Laos lay vast reaches of mountains and rivers that cut deep valleys through the High Region. There were few roads fit for vehicular traffic, and dense jungles hid almost everything from sight from the air. The population was mostly a polyglot of hill tribes, some of whom supported the French, some the Vietminh.

From the beginning the French units would struggle against the terrain and a climate that produced many types of tropical diseases. The Vietminh units suffered to a lesser degree, having learned better to cope through becoming more naturally inured to the hardships. Legendary French initiative and resourcefulness were sorely tested under these conditions, and the mobility of French units was severely handicapped. When the French were able to find enemy regional or main-force units in a situation in which superior mobility and firepower could be brought to bear, the results were often catastrophic for the enemy. But airborne battalions were the only forces that could quickly reach out beyond the Red River Delta. And once dropped, those battalions could be retrieved only by landing the same type of aircraft on an improved landing strip, not to be found in that country. Trucking or walking great distances for retrieval was not feasible or often not even possible. Additionally, modern ground and air mobility and firepower requires a huge logistical tail. The Vietminh units, increasingly well equipped with simple but effective weapons, had proven that once given a direction and objective they could get there by whatever means, on foot or sometimes by water, and they could be supplied by transportation as simple as a bicycle loaded with hundreds of pounds of supplies and munitions and pushed along crude jungle trails by one person, or by a sampan or raft packed with equipment, gliding unseen under overhanging branches.

It is probably not too severe to say that France after World War II was suffering from an acute condition of conscience, having been overrun by the Germans and governed by a Vichy regime both in France and Indochina. The heroic achievements of French men and women during the Resistance and the laudatory performance of Free French units during the Allied invasion of Europe could not lift the national spirit. Postwar politics were impossible. Since war's end, by late 1949, the Fourth Republic had seen eight changes in heads of government. The Indochina "problem," as it often was called, was draining the economy, battlefield casualties increasingly were causing deep anguish at home, and opposition to the war was growing.

From late 1949 to mid-1950, though, international events seemed to promise some help, finally, from the United States for those Frenchmen who believed they were fighting a lonesome battle against communism. An aging, sick Roosevelt had wavered between condemning France's colonial efforts and verbally backing some aspects of it. Truman in the beginning basically had not much interest in becoming involved. But when in October 1949 a victorious Mao Tse-tung proclaimed a People's Republic of China, and in January 1950 China and the Soviet Union officially recognized Ho's Democratic Republic of Vietnam, and then in June North Korea invaded South Korea, the American government began to see the French as an important bulwark against communism. From that point forward, American military and economic aid grew. At least now French units could look forward to replacing worn-out American World War II gear with much better equipment and logistics support.

But good equipment in the pipeline does not automatically translate into improved conditions on the battlefield. The year 1950, when Geneviève de Galard was receiving her nursing diploma, proved to be a tough one for the French in Tonkin. Despite some local successes, many heavily fortified outposts had to be evacuated under ferocious Vietminh assaults. In October Giap conducted his first all-out offensive throughout Vietnam, in many places with alarming success. At the end of 1950, though, the arrival of General Jean de Lattre in the combined post of high commissioner and commander in chief uplifted spirits. He stabilized the situation and started bringing some battlefield successes, beginning with January 1951 battles at Vinh Yen, northwest of Hanoi. Additionally he gave impetus to recruiting and training Vietnamese for combat. Some units, well led, were excellent, but overall during the course of the war the results were disappointing. Tragically, in May 1951, the general's only son, a young officer in Tonkin, was killed, and in less than a year the general himself was dead of cancer.

After de Lattre a succession of military commanders in Vietnam and heads of government in France did little to change the course of the war as the Vietminh were steadily gaining strength. In contrast to revolving-door French military and political leadership, the Vietminh achieved unity. Ho was the only DRV president until his death in 1969 and Giap the only commander in chief until the Americans too had been forced out of Vietnam.

In late 1952, when Geneviève was in training to become a flight nurse, Giap was moving three of his best divisions out of the Red River Delta northwest toward the T'ai High Region. This offensive seems to have had three objectives: to "liberate" the northwestern region, to threaten Laos, and to draw French units away from the delta and disperse them in difficult terrain where they could be attacked and destroyed. To counter the threat, de Lattre's successor, General Raoul Salan, initiated the concept of the *base aéroterrestre*, a distant air-ground base with a usable landing strip that could be improved and was placed in a strategic location out of which his forces could reconnoiter and attack enemy units, diminishing the threat of a move on Laos. He put the first such base at Na San in a small valley opening, some 150 air miles west of Hanoi. Geneviève was to become intimately familiar with Na San some months later, when she would fly several missions into it to evacuate wounded troops.

Salan's air-ground base at Na San turned out to be not much of a threat to Giap's units. First, the French forces had a terrible time trying to reconnoiter in the difficult terrain surrounding it, and they suffered significant casualties from encounters with the enemy. Second, the Vietminh showed they could flow around this base through the jungle, seemingly at will.

Salan had intended to create a large reserve in the delta by drawing down units outside that critical area and then using them to attack Vietminh-held areas in both eastern and northern Tonkin and in northern

Annam. This concept was a contradiction that would bedevil him and his successor. There were never enough ground or air resources to attack and simultaneously conduct successful long-term defensive pacification operations in which security for the population had to be attained if any true progress were to be achieved.

On May 5, 1953, Geneviève arrived in Hanoi during her first three-month tour of duty in Indochina. Two days later in Paris, Prime Minister René Mayer appointed Lieutenant General Henri Navarre as commander in chief for Indochina, the seventh general to serve in that post in the eight years of the Indochina War. Mayer's charge to Navarre seems to have been vague, essentially to go there and create conditions of strength from which France could negotiate an end to this endless war. And by the way, don't expect any reinforcements or an increase in budget.

Navarre had been a cavalryman in World War I, an intelligence officer for the Free French in World War II, and in the last months of that war, the commander of an armored regiment. Postwar he had commanded an armored division in occupied Germany and been on the NATO staff. He had no experience in Indochina and was replacing the highly experienced General Salan. For his commander in the North, Navarre selected Major General René Cogny, an artilleryman who had commanded a division in Tonkin. In July the French government changed for the eighteenth time in the war, and the new prime minister, Joseph Laniel, had no more concrete mission or any more substantial combat support for Navarre than had his predecessor.

Salan left Navarre a plan for a *base aéroterrestre* at Dien Bien Phu, and on July 25, 1953, Navarre issued orders for its seizure, a key step in what came to be known as the Navarre Plan. For his base commander, Navarre chose another cavalryman, Colonel Christian de Castries, who had significant command experience in Tonkin. The combination of Cogny and de Castries seemed ideal—firepower of artillery, mobility of cavalry. Dien Bien Phu, about eleven miles long and five miles wide, was one of the very few valleys—indeed, the largest one—in northwest Tonkin that was open enough to accommodate a large force. An added benefit was that it produced much of the rice that supported the Vietminh troops in the High Region. On the map it appeared that its seizure could seriously handicap Giap's operations there and his move on Laos.

Dien Bien Phu had already played a prominent role in the French-Indochina wars. After the Japanese coup, much of the Tonkin garrison was able to fight a delaying action back to DBP and remain there, using the grass airstrip, for almost two months before having to withdraw into China. Later the CLI inserted a team there to recruit the hill tribesman. And later still Salan had put a small garrison there but had to remove it under pressure in November 1952, intending to return and make it a significant *base aéroterrestre* when he could accumulate enough forces to do so.

Strong objections were raised to Navarre's decision to act upon Salan's plan. Some French army officers said that the Viets could go wherever they wanted to go, support themselves in doing so, and cause great mischief. Especially urgent warnings were raised by the French air force, which pointed out that DBP was 180 air miles from Hanoi and would require an enormous amount of resources to provide the air strike and air lift capacities that would no doubt be required—this at the same time Navarre was directing that other operations be launched in Tonkin and as far south as central Annam, all of which had to be supported from Hanoi.

The counterargument was Na San. When it had been attacked the previous December, it had held and caused the enemy heavy casualties. Navarre discounted the base commander's blunt statements that this had resulted only partly from good French soldiering and the rest from the sheer luck of missteps by the enemy. And when in August 1953 Na San was successfully evacuated under pressure in order to concentrate the reserves, this seemed to the Navarre air-conditioned headquarters in far away Saigon assurance that DBP would succeed in putting a huge dent in Giap's plans.

However, neither Navarre nor Cogny had envisioned that Giap could move five divisions into position around the DBP defenders, little damaged by the many air strikes directed against them; or that they could be supported by masses of laborers building roads and trails for artillery and supplies; or that when French battalions moved out of DBP on reconnaissance in force missions they would encounter inordinately tough going in the difficult terrain and incur heavy casualties; or that the Viet artillery could be dug into the forward slopes of the hills surrounding DBP to provide massive direct fire onto the airfield and deadly antiaircraft fire against the planes trying to land or drop men and supplies; or, incredibly, that this enemy artillery could survive massive counterbattery fire and air strikes and itself become dominant.

Long before Geneviève was trapped in Dien Bien Phu, French forces —army, navy, air force—had proven they were tough fighters of the highest quality. All elements of those forces—French regulars, Colonial Infantry, Legionnaires, Africans and North Africans, and the Vietnamese, Cambodians, and Laotians integrated into these units—had shown those who were watching and interested that France could match any other troops in the world in courage and steadfast determination. It was the fate of one person, though, to reveal dramatically that French women also had those same brave qualities during critical times—as well as the compassion and solace that only a woman can offer. That one person was the sole French woman during those terrible days of Dien Bien Phu, Geneviève de Galard.

—*Col. William C. Haponski*, USA (Ret.)

Note: Col. William C. Haponski is the author of *One Hell of a Ride: Inside an Armored Cavalry Task Force in Vietnam.*

Mother and me. *Private collection of the author*

My father. *Private collection of the author*

Chateau de Terraube, ancestral estate of the Galard family. *Private collection of the author*

Chateau de Labatut, where I spent my vacations as a child. *Estate of the author's grandmother*

On the steps of Labatut with my sister and cousins. *Private collection of the author*

I always tried to do as well as Marie-Suzanne, my older sister. *Private collection of the author*

At twenty I dreamed of other horizons. *Private collection of the author*

My first mission as flight nurse in Tunisia. *Private collection of the author*

Operation Castor, November 20, 1954. *ECPAD*

Installation of the entrenched camp. *ECPAD*

On an embankment at Dien Bien Phu in March 1954, some days before the big attack.
Private collection of the author

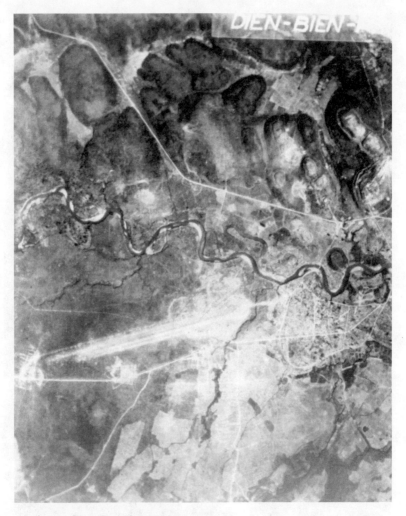

Aerial view of Dien Bien Phu. *ECPAD*

Embarkment of the wounded by Dakotas under Vietminh fire, 1954. *ECPAD*

Chapter One

ROOTS

"Actually, I am not unhappy that you are in DBP; at least you are not in danger of crashing in a plane."

If things had not been so bad, I would have burst out laughing at this letter from my mother in the mail parachuted into the camp in April 1954. But the arrival of the mailbag, the only thread still connecting us to our families in the heat of battle, represented a moment too anxiously anticipated and too emotional to feel like laughing. In fact, I felt relieved to think that my mother, for the time being, was not cruelly worried, she who had a phobia of planes and was so easily anxious since my father's death.

My happy childhood had been turned upside down in 1934, when I was nine years old, by the loss of my father, whom I adored. Many images come back to me as I remember this beloved father, gone at fifty-five from complications of what was discreetly referred to as "a long illness." We had been living for several years in Paris, in a lively part of the 17th Arrondissement not far from the market in rue de Levis, on a pleasant private lane in the apartment where I still reside today with my husband. When I was five my father would accompany me to school on the other side of Place Malesherbes, which was quite unusual for a man of his generation. He would hold me affectionately by the hand and always carried my book bag. I was filled with all the pride in the world when I walked alongside this man with the powerful and self-contained carriage. I loved his blue eyes, his clear glance, his sensitivity.

Then the illness came. For three years my mother never left my father's side. I shall never forget the morning when my mother came to fetch us in our room, my sister, Marie-Suzanne, and I, so that we could give him a last kiss.

Stricken in her deepest core, my mother lived this trial in her faith. She rarely expressed her feelings, but she lived for us. Perhaps, in her fear of something happening to us, she was somewhat overprotective. That was understandable. She had waited ten years without children, and our older sister had died the day after her birth. As was the custom then, my mother strictly observed her mourning, and we, two little girls, would have preferred her to dress in more cheerful colors.

During our father's illness we often were placed in the care of our governess, Victorine Honoré. "Torine" had come to us when I was two years old and was completely part of the family. I loved her tenderly. She could do anything; she was always welcoming and full of affection. She had grown up in a large family from Brittany and was the aunt of the future Cardinal Jean Honoré. Many years later, long after my return from Dien Bien Phu, Monseigneur Honoré, at that time archbishop of Tours, confided in me, "Aunt Torine had two loves: you and me."

With the death of my father I discovered pain, at nine years of age, and I have never forgotten it. All young children who have suffered a similar loss know what I mean. Of course, after that our life was less sunny, less lively. But our childhood continued under easy conditions as our mother's family, landowners rooted in military tradition, controlled a comfortable income.

After being widowed my mother consecrated herself almost exclusively to our education, choosing our schools with care. She had a strong sense of family, and our house was wide open to our cousins, some of whom were boarders. Her educational principles were very strict, but except for a few conventions that no longer apply, I remember none that I would eliminate today. My mother had traveled widely with her father, and she had the same concern to open our minds, but World War II restricted her projects. She gave us, by example more than by words, a sense of others. She hardly ever criticized those around her, and I only understood much later that her tolerance, sometimes surprising to the child I was, surely was her way of living her faith daily. My mother attended Mass every morning. I too was very devout. In fact, I was so immersed in that atmosphere that I did not ask myself questions. But little by little I felt the need to deepen my faith and to live it.

I was attending school at the Cours Louise-de-Bettignies, boulevard Malesherbes, now run by the Ursuline nuns, where I studied until the summer of 1939. Our headmistress, Mademoiselle Georget, would often tell us about the heroine for whom the school was named; she had been an informant in World War I for the British army in the north of France. We were shown a film depicting her arrest by the Germans in Tournai and her death in captivity in Cologne in 1918. It left in me a profound impression.

I loved going to class because I loved learning and discovering, and I was a rather good student, often first in my class, except in math. I enjoyed history, and especially geography, which we learned on immense maps, pink, blue, and green, that hung from two brass rings over the blackboard and which led us to dream of distant adventures. Already I liked organizing things. To teach us the many French departments (administrative divisions), the geography professor separated us into two teams. I volunteered to be a team leader: I would gather my friends in our apartment to "warm them up" before the test—and we won!

Despite the wound from my father's death, I was a cheerful child, spontaneous and very affectionate—somewhat shy perhaps, because at the time I had no self-confidence. I was always trying to do as well as my sister, older than I by twenty-one months. Marie-Suzanne was more independent, more enterprising, and more self-assured. She encouraged me to do amusing stunts—climb trees, do tricks on my bicycle—and I looked up to her. I wanted to measure up, to follow her, to do everything she did, and that annoyed her at times. Like the day when I was hanging upside down on the railing of a small bridge and fell into the water, on the last day of vacation, after all the suitcases had been packed.

A few years later, my sister and I were invited by friends to a fair at Polytechnic School. As we went from booth to booth we stopped before a fakir telling fortunes. That day he predicted for my sister a life full of unexpected events and for me a quiet existence. Circumstances quickly took charge in reversing our roles.

For our summer vacations, which in those days lasted three months, my mother always rented, for July and August, a villa at the seashore or in the mountains. This allowed us to discover different regions of France. In the photo album of my youth, the beaches on the Atlantic appear side by side with the Pyrenees and Alps. Then in September came the rite that we would not have missed for the world: We would go to the home of my paternal grandmother, Mélénie de Galard, and later to our uncle's home in Labatut.

If there is a place in France where the most precious memories of my childhood are gathered it is that family property in Haute-Garonne, situated on the commune of Saint-André, eighty kilometers from Toulouse, where we always ended our summers. Labatut, for me, meant the joyous reunion of cousins: the three children of my uncle Elie, my father's older brother, and the five children of my uncle Guy, his younger brother. I had always regretted having no brothers, and those holidays with my cousins helped to fill the gap. At that time my paternal grandmother still reigned over Labatut, where she would entertain her unmarried cousins during the winter months to break her solitude. She had been widowed as a very young woman, and her powerful personality gave her the strength to raise her three sons and her daughter Louise. During our vacations we always went after dinner to wish her good night in her room, where she would give us candy.

Since her death in 1930 the property had belonged to Uncle Elie, who was my godfather. There we spent vacations that were dreams come true, under the shade of the tall elms and centenarian oaks that had witnessed the passage of generations.

Is there anything more banal and at the same time more irreplaceable than these images of a happy childhood? I remember wild rides on the back of Midship, my uncle's small Arabian pony, which he would make us ride bareback, using nothing more than a blanket; great picnic expeditions in the countryside to join cousins and friends; acrobatics on bicycles down a sloping field; giant leaps off mountains of stacked hay; gathering mushrooms whose aroma filled the air; and harvesting grapes on neighboring farms. We loved to play in the orangery, where old carriages were stored. How many journeys we traveled there, giving free rein to our imagination.

Originally Labatut was an old house built in the seventeenth century, but a fire had ravaged it in 1906. It no longer had any of the cachet of its earlier days because it had been rebuilt just before the war by an architect friend of the family in the style of the large villas on the Normandy coast; esthetically, it was a little Deauville or Trouville in the Comminges.

But at the time I could not imagine anything more magnificent: the large hall with its balcony from which we performed small plays before our proud parents, the wide stone front steps where the traditional family photographs were taken, the terrace surrounded by flowers where we preferred to sit rather than in the salon, and the "priest's hat," the spot where two paths met, bordered by trees, where we staged our bicycle races.

Yes, the roots of my childhood were anchored in the southwest of France. I always treasured in my heart its landscapes, sounds, and aromas, long after our return to Paris, where the buildings and the streets suddenly seemed sad and dirty.

After the death of my father, the second trauma in my life came on September 1, 1939, the day Germany invaded Poland, starting World War II. I was fourteen and I cried. My youth had been shaped by the patriotism of my family. On both sides, paternal and maternal, I belonged to a family of military officers who truly represented an ideal of courage, a sense of duty and of service to the nation. I knew that for centuries members of my family had been ready to die in the defense of their country.

Recently one of my nephews discovered in a dresser, hidden between two drawers, a small notebook that my maternal grandmother had titled her "Confidant." In 1871, at age fifteen, she had written in it: "It is France I love best, after God. I would stop at nothing to save her, I would be happy if some day Heaven grants me the honor, the infinite joy of dying for her."

I was proud to descend from the line of the Galard Terraube; one of my ancestors had ridden in the Crusades and another had fought with Jeanne d'Arc. The Galard Terraube form the senior branch of the Galard family, one of the oldest in the history of France, as far back as Clovis in the sixth century. I was proud and at the same time eager to prove myself worthy of these famous individuals who had proved their loyalty to their Christian faith, to their native soil, to a spirit of service and honor. It was not an imaginary world but the living example of generations that had formed my youth. For me World War I was not a vague memory but a living history. My father, a reserve officer; his two brothers, both career officers; and many cousins had distinguished themselves in 1914–18, and two cousins had been killed.

On my mother's side I had the example of my aunt Suzanne, who joined the Red Cross and died of tuberculosis. My mother often spoke to me of this only sister whom she cherished, and I could not ignore the photograph of her group of young volunteer nurses, always placed on the mantelpiece of Mother's room. Did she play a role in my own vocation? I could not say, but sometimes the paths of our imagination decide for us.

On that first day of September 1939 we were at Labatut for our summer vacation. My mother, worried about the bombardments on Paris, soon decided to move with her daughters to Toulouse. The first winter was bearable. Mother had found a large apartment on rue de Metz, in the very center of the "Ville Rose." But a year later its owners, a doctor and his family, returned and we moved out. As all the refugees were flowing south into the free zone allowed by the Germans in agreement with the Vichy government, it became difficult to find an apartment. We finally landed a nice one, on the second floor, which was referred to in those days (with a certain condescension that shocks us today) as the domestics' quarters. It was not at all comfortable. One day mice ate our ration cards, and we had to request new ones.

Materially, as for most of the French, those years were very difficult. My sister and I, both adolescents, experienced privations, hunger, and cold. To that period I probably owe the physical and mental strength that helped me bear challenges, both at Dien Bien Phu and along my life's path. We had no central heat. My sister and I always studied in our coats and gloves. The two stoves, in our room and in the dining room, barely maintained the thermometer at 14 degrees Celsius. My mother, who only had a chimney in her room, would wake in the morning to 7 degrees of temperature. It was under these conditions that in Toulouse I passed my first and then my second baccalaureate in 1941 and in 1942. My mother had chosen our school very carefully. I spent the last three years of my schooling at the Dominican Sisters of the Holy Name of Jesus.

Because of the war our diversions were rare. Our mother, anxious to develop our musical knowledge, took us to the Capitole to hear comic-operas: *Carmen*, *The Marriage of Figaro*, *The Tales of Hoffmann*. Sixty years later I remember as an exception the breath of fresh air and of mirth brought by Charles Trenet, the famous singer and songwriter, during an unforgettable performance he gave in Toulouse before a full house. We were not isolated because many of our cousins lived in the southwest. The nearness of Labatut made it easy to go there for all our vacations and to reunite with our family on a regular basis.

I became increasingly attached to the countryside of this corner of the Comminges, which consisted of hills parallel to the Pyrenees mostly covered with woods and of the valleys that were fully cultivated. Essentially rural, the Comminges preserves many facets of our history. I would find in the Save Valley the prehistoric vestiges of Neanderthal man, who lived 130,000 years before Christ, but only nine kilometers from Labatut, in Aurignac, we would visit the cave where Aurignacian man lived, 35,000 years before Christ. Nearby in Alan, the ancient bishops' palace hid a small marvel. The tympanus of its ogival door presents the famous cow of the Béarn, sculpted with vigor and elegance. We loved hearing the story of the courageous inhabitants who, in the late fifteenth century, rang the bells and arrived with their pitchforks to chase away the workers who were about to dismantle the famous artwork for an antiquarian wanting to sell it in the United States.

From Labatut we would bicycle regularly to Terraube, a castle built around 1272 for the de Galard family, dukes of Gascony, enlarged in the sixteenth and seventeenth centuries. Ever since, except for the period of the French Revolution, Terraube has belonged to the Galard family. Since 1947 it has been listed as a historical monument by the government. My father spent all his vacations at Terraube, which was his grandparents' home. Twice I spent a month of summer holidays there with my sister and my first cousin, Madeleine. This house rich with history pulled us back into the past. For centuries our family and the people of this fortified village in the Gers were permanently connected. A tapestry adorned one wall of the grand salon. It depicted the court of Louis XI, with his lords represented as figures in a set of cards, at the time the game was invented. The jack of diamonds pictured Hector de Galard, appointed in 1479 *grand maréchal des logis* (field marshal of the king's camps and dwellings). (Even today in France the jack of diamonds is still named Hector.) He was surrounded by the most illustrious names of his era. It is in memory of this legendary ancestor that the Galards from different branches regularly choose the name Hector for their firstborn sons.

We also would bicycle to Lasalle in the Gers, where my uncle Guy lived, a colonel in the French air force. On arriving, my sister and I were proud of having ridden over a dozen summits of the Gascogne hills. My aunt lived there without electricity and insisted on giving us butter, which we took turns beating by hand, and flour. Gasoline was hard to come by, and my aunt often would travel about in a horse-drawn carriage. I loved accompanying her as sometimes she would let me hold the reins.

At the end of 1942, worried by the Allied invasion of North Africa so close off the coast of southern France, the Germans extended their occupation of France to its southern zone. Since at the time the Germans were everywhere in France, at the end of the school year in summer 1943 we returned to our apartment in Paris, which was much more comfortable. In the capital the first priority was survival and the essential preoccupation was the procurement of food. We had the good luck to be provisioned by Victorine's family in Brittany, who would regularly send us meat and butter. To buy vegetables everyone had to stand in line. On finding out that a shipment of vegetables was due the next day, we would take a folding stool and relay each other every two hours, from five in the morning on, to bring home two kilos of carrots and a head of lettuce. With my sister, I wandered also through the fields in the outskirts of Paris, around Longjumeau and Sceaux. We bought a good amount of vegetables from the local growers, bringing home all we could carry on our bicycles.

In 1943–44 we lived through the bombardments, causing hurried descent into the cellar at the first sound of the siren. One gets used to anything, and we were not afraid. The shelters seemed very sturdy. In fact, I believe that I have rarely been afraid; perhaps it is a certain lack of awareness or a family trait? When one's ancestors have overcome innumerable and cruel challenges, it seems natural to adjust to troubled times. Between air-raid alerts, I would ride my bicycle around Paris, either to the Sorbonne for English classes or to the dispensary in the 18th Arrondissement, managed by Sister St. Arcade, a friend of my mother, where my sister and I would weigh the newborns. That is when I became involved in several associations and volunteer organizations. I worked in a hospital with young handicapped patients, trying to get them to accomplish weaving projects that would provide them with an income. There I discovered the immense challenge in making the work of the handicapped profitable for them because of their limited strength and physical disabilities. (Since then subsidized centers have been developed that address that challenge.)

Our return to Paris awakened me to politics. In Toulouse we had followed closely the Nazis' actions. We had been horrified by the imposition of yellow stars on the Jewish population, but we had trouble catching the British radio news and, like the majority of the French, I did not hear, for instance, General de Gaulle's rallying call of June 18. Besides, there were few members of the French Resistance around me. Before the debacle my family was—in the spirit of the time—supportive of Marshal

Henri-Philippe Pétain, the hero of Verdun. But everything changed for us when he allowed the Germans to dictate his positions. Thus we reflected the fluctuations of our compatriots.

Until the summer of 1943 we lived in the province in an exclusively feminine milieu, our mother already being elderly. We did not really learn about the history of the Resistance and of the Free French forces, based in London, until the last months of the war. Coming back to Paris, we started to react as we listened every day to British radio. We followed closely the progress of the troops and we experienced the anxiety, then the joyous intoxication, of the Allied landing at Normandy.

On Liberation Day, August 25, 1944, as soon as we learned that General Philippe Leclerc was in Paris and that de Gaulle was going to arrive on the Champs-Élysées, my sister and I started off toward the Place de l'Étoile. We took shelter under porches when snipers on the rooftops started shooting before rushing on toward our destination. I felt very proud to have arrived at last at the foot of the Arc de Triomphe, but my joy was suddenly spoiled. I was stupefied by the attitude of Parisians who were cursing the driver of a German truck whose dead comrade leaned on his shoulder. My compatriots were confusing these soldiers with the Nazis who had given them orders. Further on, people were insulting women with shaven heads who were being driven by in another truck. From the hecklers' faces there emanated such hatred that it made me ache, despite the errors of these women. I was nineteen and suddenly I was discovering hatred and intolerance.

After VE day, May 8, 1945, social life returned very quickly, especially in Paris. My sister and I went out a lot to make up for the austere years we had recently lived. Marie-Suzanne was engaged the following year and married in 1947. As for myself, I had passed my certificates of practical studies and of English literature. I had a busy life, but I still lacked a true guiding vision.

That is when I decided to take a new path. The English studies I had pursued were for my personal interest, and I was realizing that continuing in that direction could not fill my life. I dreamed of new perspectives, fewer self-centered adventures. Quite simply I wanted to be useful, and I could not fathom a life without giving to others or pursuing some ideal. Besides, having grown up surrounded with tenderness and solicitude, although somewhat overly protected by my anxious mother, I craved to discover wider horizons.

Armed with my two certificates in English, in 1949 I decided to prepare the diploma for medical-social work, followed in 1950 by the nursing diploma, which would lead to what I believed to be my vocation.

During those years I used my vacations to discover the countries that attracted me: Italy, Spain, and Norway. I had always loved geography, and from the time of my adolescence I dreamed of going to the French colonies of Morocco and Indochina.

As for Morocco, it was easy. I left with a group of young people by ship in fourth class. I was enthused by this journey: the beauty of the countryside, the architectural marvels, the medinas bursting with life, the colors, the scents. Such a totally different environment cannot leave one indifferent. My strongest memory was that of the fantasias of Moulay-Idriss, the holy city where we had the luck to arrive in time for the annual festivities, even if we did feel somewhat like trespassers on the people's revelry. On our return passage we decorated part of the storeroom with our purchases—carpets and ottomans, copper trays and ceramics—to entertain the captain, who invited us to a party enlivened by the brother of Henri Salvador, also a singer, and all his troupe.

In Indochina the war had been releasing all its violence since 1945. In March a Japanese coup resulted in the imprisonment of the French military and elimination of French civil authority. This encouraged the declarations of independence hoped for by the five Indochinese territories. But although the Communists cleverly maneuvered to seize power, France was unable to close off the colonial era by preparing to grant the unavoidable independence. Beginning in September, after the capitulation of Japan, the first Free French forces returned to Saigon and, initially under British control, began to try to control that city and the surrounding territory. Ho Chi Minh, after the failed attempts to reach an agreement at Fontainebleau, decided to fight for his country's autonomy, and insurrection in Hanoi started on December 19, 1946. After 1950, for the Vietnamese, the war was definitely a civil war, as tragic as the Spanish Civil War of 1937 had been. Many in the free world also saw it as a front for the containment of international communism.

I felt drawn by this distant colony, which had become, since the 1930s, a virtual myth for many Frenchmen. The conflict there had caused many casualties. A friend's brother, on leave, told me stories of his life and of the role he played on a post near the Chinese border. He was killed two months after his return to Indochina for a second round of duty.

Through the newspaper reports we followed anxiously the drama of Colonial Route 4, the disaster of Cao Bang, the evacuation of Langson. In January 1951 the arrival of General de Lattre de Tassigny brought victories and new hope.

I wanted to leave for Indochina after my nursing studies, but my sister had followed her husband, an officer in Germany, and I felt I had no right to leave France for a long stay, leaving our mother alone when she was starting to lose her sight.

Providentially, at the same time I ran into a childhood friend, Marie-Rose Calmettes, who had been my classmate at the Cours Louise-de-Bettignies. I shared my scruples with her. Her response filled me with joy: "Papa is also widowed, and I didn't want to leave him alone for two years. I chose to join the Flight Nurses because our missions bring us regularly back to Paris."

This is how I first heard about Convoyeuses de l'Air, the flight nurses of the Groupement des Moyens Militaires Transports Aériens, or GM-MTA (the transport air service of the French air force). These flying nurses had been traveling for several years on the planes to Africa and Indochina, transporting military families, evacuating the wounded and the sick. They signed two-year contracts with the French air force, but between assignments they were stationed in Paris. Of course, to join, one needed to have a state nursing diploma and pass an examination.

The decision was important. I wanted to take some time to reflect on it in silence and in prayer because my faith had always held a central place in my life. I needed a real "rendezvous" with myself.

The Benedictine convent and its lovely chapel in Vanves, a suburb south of Paris where I spent thirty-six hours, gave me at once the serenity I needed to think and the presence of a nun who was always available for guidance. On Monday morning my choice was made. I was going for it and would present myself at the next exam. I had no idea how this decision was going to turn my life upside down.

Chapter Two

DREAMS OF INDOCHINA

My worries were over. I had passed the test to become a flight nurse. I felt a profound joy, a fulfillment such as one experiences in youth when life bends to one's desire. At last I would be able to accomplish my vocation.

For some unknown reason the test, usually administered in May, was not given in the spring of 1952 and was rescheduled for that autumn. Having reached my decision at the last minute, I had barely two months to "cram" without interruption. The other two candidates were a pilot and a paratrooper. I was the ugly duckling who had never set foot in an airplane. From then on, having enlisted in the flight nurses, I was to remain part of the French air force for a long time.

EARLY FLIGHT NURSE DAYS

It was of Indochina that I could dream at last. My fellow trainees, Jaic and Alberte, were both fine young women and morally sound. Despite our individual characters, we have always remained very close. In these last days of 1952, we were filled with the same desire to serve and to be worthy of our predecessors.

Some had already distinguished themselves in Indochina and had gone through very dangerous situations, particularly in September–October 1950. Colonial Route 4, which ran along the border with China through a thick jungle and over mountainous terrain, had nonetheless been chosen as the evacuation route for the posts of Cao Bang near the border and Dong Khe, forty-five kilometers farther south. However, a massive Vietminh attack wiped out one column of French soldiers coming up from That Khe and another column coming down from Cao Bang to meet them. Four thousand of our men were lost.

In late October the Viet commander ordered a three-day cease-fire to allow retrieval of the wounded. "The landing field," said Valerie, one of the veteran nurses who took part in that operation, "was short, bumpy, damaged by the rains, and only one part of the strip was usable. The second risk was what the Vietminh would do when they had our planes at their mercy." As yet no Junker had landed on that field. The Ju 52 was an odd aircraft made of corrugated metal, uncomfortable but very strong, built for short-hop flights with a maximum speed of 250 kilometers per hour. Its landing gear was not retractable, and its principal advantage was its ability to land anywhere.

Fortunately the pilot, a curious and engaging individual nicknamed the "Baron," was a crack figure in the air force. Upon landing the atmosphere was tense. "As we set foot on land," continued our friend Valerie, "and looked up, we noticed five or six Viet sentries, machine guns on their hips in firing position. We did not dare move a finger." The wounded she and another nurse managed to recover that day were in an unbelievable state. They were living skeletons, pale, with wounds and broken bones put together with minimal dressings, rudimentary splints, and plaster casts. They had been left several days without care.

Another cease-fire was agreed to in early November 1950 in Langson, but as the evacuation plane was landing almost vertically, the Vietminh antiaircraft started shooting and the pilot had to return to Hanoi where the mechanic counted a dozen hits on the fuselage. Long after, our friend Valerie learned that the first cease-fire granted by the Vietminh had been to halt all French military action and to allow the Viets to move their troops and mass them elsewhere.

In October 1951, at the time of the first Vietminh raid on Nghia Lo, the perilous evacuations in the "high country" of Tonkin earned two flight nurses the honor of being decorated at the scene of the battle. Hoa Binh and Na San were other sites where the nurses and the air crews, with modesty and selflessness, took enormous risks in order to evacuate the wounded.

With the carefree optimism of youth, death was certainly not on my mind at that time, although several of our seniors had already perished on duty. Lucienne Just died in June 1947 in the crash of a Junker in the area of Djiring, a high Indochinese plateau. Cecile Idrac had already been shot at and wounded in May 1947, only to die in the fiery crash of a Halifax in September 1949 in Gabon, Africa. Béatrice de L'Épine was twenty-two years old when she met her death in the mountainous region of Cambodia named the Mountain of the Elephant.

In July 1951 the plane to which Geneviève Roure was assigned crashed on takeoff in Gao, a town in present-day Mali. She was able to move her passengers rapidly into the tail of the plane. Although already terribly burned, she climbed back into the aircraft to save two more. At Niamey she helped nurse the wounded before falling into a coma and dying a few hours later.

My fellow trainee, Jaic, met her death on duty in Algeria aboard a helicopter into which she had just settled an injured patient. My other training companion, Alberte, having returned to civilian life after her marriage, was piloting a private plane in France when she was caught in a thunderstorm and hit a high-tension wire. Out of our initial trio in January 1953, when we entered the French air force, I remain the only survivor.

One of the mysteries of war is that it seems quite natural to those fighting in it. Our seriousness was a reflection of the situation, but it was mingled with a carefree lack of consciousness. Action mesmerized us.

In my first month of service, I received both theoretical and practical training. During my maiden flight on a Junker, I felt a heady sensation on takeoff, even on that old bird. I marveled at the houses and the square fields that were becoming smaller and smaller as we pulled away. Later we practiced emergency evacuations in case of a crash or forced landing. This time we flew on a Dakota. The famous C-47 Douglas Dakota had been the most frequently used aircraft during World War II and the wars that followed. A strong two-engine plane, it had a large side door that allowed for all sorts of cargo as well as the dropping of paratroopers. It was often equipped to transport twenty-four wounded lying on stretchers.

My first real mission with passengers brought me to Tunis. I was accompanied by an old-timer, nicknamed "Boum," whose duty was to observe me and confirm my capacity to be a flight nurse. We left Paris in the fog and did not emerge from it until we were over the Alps. The sight was dazzling: the snowy summits sparkled under the sun as they surged out of a sea of clouds.

On my second assignment I accompanied Colonel de la Chenelière, commander of the GMMTA (Air Transport Command), and his staff, who were on their way to inspect several bases in central Africa. This was a long itinerary from Paris that took us first to Oran, where we exchanged our "maritime" gear (dinghies and life jackets) for our "Sahara" gear, which allowed one to survive a crash in mid-desert, thanks to our load of jerrycans full of water. Our trip went on through Nouasseur, Tindouf, Dakar, Thies, Labe, Bamako, Gao, Aoulef, Algiers, and back to Paris.

This rather special mission turned out to be disappointing since the passengers did not need my care. My work consisted mostly of providing sandwiches to the crew, all of whom had an insatiable appetite. It was my first contact with the Sahara, its immense stretches of sand, its dunes as far as the eye could see. In Tindouf, in the extreme southwest of Algeria, the heat was stifling. From Thies, in Senegal, I was able to get to Dakar, its capital, a city both industrial and mercantile with its own university and its large harbor, protected at its mouth by the Île de Gorée. I also visited its old city, rich in history and ancient military installations. At Bamako and Gao, located on the left bank of the Niger, I was enchanted by the river, a long silver thread that crosses the Sahel Desert, on which the silhouettes of boatmen paddling against the current stood out against the sunset. At Alouef, in the immensity of the desert, I saw appear out of nowhere Arab children offering sand roses (hardened sand resembling roses found in the desert).

In Algiers the crew did not leave the field, and this time we replaced our Sahara gear with the maritime equipment. After we took off, the view over the magnificent bay made me suddenly want to come back to it. Nevertheless, the essential part of my vocation as a flight nurse was to be played in Indochina.

INDOCHINA AT LAST

I went to Indochina for the first time at the end of April 1953—for only three months because we were flying constantly and were assigned to accompany servicemen being repatriated to France. But those three months were to be busy.

I boarded the prestigious Sky, the DC4 assigned to official personnel, which brought us to Saigon in thirty-six hours with only four stops: Nicosia, Karachi, Delhi, and Calcutta. It was in that last city that I had my first contact with the misery and mendicant ways of the children. I was deeply moved to see them brandish their stumps in the midst of traffic jams in which luxurious cars mingled with pitiful carts among the sacred cows. The monsoon had started, and that day curtains of water fell suddenly on the town. The rains did not last long, but they were spectacular. Right after they stopped, steam started rising from the ground, bringing back the oppressive heat.

When I landed in Saigon, after a tiring flight, I was struck by the intense, humid heat. Fortunately one of my fellow flight nurses met me at the plane, and I was quickly taken in charge by one of my cousins, who took me to visit the entire city.

I was fascinated to discover this large city built in European style in a tropical landscape, with its districts of comfortable villas surrounded by verandahs in luxuriant and well-maintained gardens; its wide avenues bordered with sycamores or rubber trees; its pink cathedral crowned by two soaring steeples; its majestic white governor's palace encircled by an immense garden filled with flamboyants, frangipaniers, and multicolored flower beds; its rue Catinat, running between lovely European-style boutiques and shaded by tamarind trees; and its Continental Hotel, with its terrace, in these years of war, as famous as the best known Parisian cafés. A few kilometers from deadly battles taking place all over Indochina, the residents of Saigon continued to exist in an atmosphere of dolce vita that seemed to me bizarre.

I was further amazed on arriving at Saigon's port, where the sampans glided silently in front of the wooden pier at the Point of the Jokers. Our tour extended to Cholon, the Chinese city teeming with life. From every alley came the odors of cooking food, prepared in the street by ambulant merchants. The aromas of *nuoc mam* and Chinese soup mingled with scents of sandalwood and incense. I was intoxicated by all these aromas, the spices and perfumes of the Orient of which I had dreamed so long. I admired the young Vietnamese women in their *ao dai*, a long tunic worn over trousers, who had no trouble maneuvering their bicycles among thousands of cycle-rickshaws.

I was quickly assigned to Hanoi to join the northern detachment. After the heat of Saigon, the climate of Hanoi felt delicious. But I was mostly happy to be sent to Tonkin so soon, where the heaviest fighting was taking place.

I had not expected, however, to be thrown into war so quickly. I arrived in Hanoi on May 5, 1953, and took off again to accompany a flight nurse to Luang Prabang in Laos. We were to evacuate a number of soldiers who had tramped through the brush on an exhausting march of sixty kilometers. They were the survivors of battles at Sam Neua and of the entire region around Luang Prabang. The lovely royal city, with its charming pagodas lining the main street, seemed relatively calm, but the surrounding brush was being cleared to avoid a surprise attack. This mountainous and wooded region was indeed quite danger- ous, as each cluster of trees could provide cover for an ambush. That same day we also landed in Vientiane. During the following days, these evacuation missions took me to Xieng Khouang and to the Plain of Jars, where many battles were occurring.

Thus I discovered, from Hanoi on, the minutely regulated life of a flight nurse attached to the northern area. We had no time to sit around. Each morning we climbed by jeep to the military airfield of Bach Mai, which was secured by Moroccan sentries. We took off on the first avail- able aircraft, be it civilian or military, to evacuate casualties in whatever direction our team leader had designated. Later, in 1954, the military flights were only on Dakota C-47s. These planes were more spacious, faster, and quieter than the Junkers. They were well adapted for medical evacuations.

The rainy season had come early and the planes were not always allowed to take off, as the low ceiling and the tenacious fog made fly- ing too dangerous. We would then return to the small villa, humid and uncomfortable, where we were quartered, located in an alley opening on the boulevard Gambetta.

On my first day of rest, I left our villa to wander in the city of Hanoi. Everyone spoke of the charming Petit Lac, and I was eager to discover it. Leaving behind me the theater, I proceeded along rue Paul-Bert, thread- ing my way through all the bicycles. When I arrived at Petit Lac, I was enchanted by a flower market, its stands spilling with color, and on the mirror of the water, a small pagoda. The light shadows of the trees along its shores and the reflections of clouds passing over the water enhanced the charm and the life that imbued the whole. I would return some eve- nings to pass young lovers drawn by this romantic spot and admire the young girls in their spotless *ao dai*, with their long black hair drawn back on the nape of their necks. But that day I continued my way toward the old Vietnamese quarter: the Street of Silk and the Street of Cotton, their display windows glistening with color under the shade of the flamboyant trees. Enveloped in the scent of the Orient, the women went about under their conical hats, bearing their pendulums across their shoulders. They trotted along in their typical mincing steps, carrying large baskets of fruit or vegetables. Most of them wore black satin pajamas with short white vests. A long tress of hair enclosed in a black band of fabric circled their heads. Men passed by, carrying on their balancing poles all they needed to prepare *pho*, a soup of rice noodles flavored with strips of meat and served in a highly spiced bouillon. They would stop on request.

I felt so far from the battles. Hanoi was the place of relaxation for the warrior. Our friends, soldiers or officers posted at Na San, were delighted when they were on leave to rest and to go out with the flight nurses. We would go with them for a drink at the well-known bars of the Metropole Hotel or the Splendide, where the air transport crews would take us at the end of a very intense day. In those places, since the start of the war, one would run into an animated and cosmopolitan clientele of many journalists and writers from Europe or America covering the Indochina conflict, including Jean Larteguy, Jules Roy, Graham Green, Lucien Bodard, Max Olivier-Lacamp, Max Clos, Fred Spark, and Jean-François Chauvel.

On off-duty days, quite rare, I sometimes tasted the pleasures of sailing on the Grand Lac. This was another sort of experience. On its shore Japanese lilacs waved their blue flowers, and as one left the land behind, the landscape and the total silence transported one far from the city. Sunshine and a breeze, what peace!

At that time the medical evacuation missions would take us regularly toward Lai Chau, to the northwest of Hanoi in the high country. I never ceased admiring the view when the aircraft flew, hedge-hopping, over the Claveau Pass before making a 45-degree right turn to start down the valley toward the airfield at its other end. Along the road that skirted the field, T'ai women walked in single file at their graceful pace, so elegant in their traditional costume, a white top held close by silver hooks, a long skirt of dark fabric, a wide, flat straw hat.

I also enjoyed going to Lai Chau because its medical post was directed by Doctor (Major) Millon, whom we called the "Toubib." He was a great friend to the flight nurses. We all found him likable and warm, and he always knew how to explain clearly what we needed to do. One day a skirmish took place thirty kilometers from Lai Chau and the Vietminh cut off the road. A helicopter was preparing to take off, but visibility was bad due to the rains, interfering with the evacuation of the wounded.

During the wait I drove by jeep with Toubib to visit the sick in the valley. One old T'ai woman refused to be taken to Lanessan Hospital in Hanoi. We entered her house built on pilings. The whole family lived there *pêle-mêle,* with the old woman and two small babies sleeping naked in a corner. On the way back we stopped at a post, partly underground. It was held by a *goum,* a company of Moroccans who had built themselves a small chapel where the chaplain of Lai Chau came every Sunday to offer Mass. The men were not in the regular army, but Moroccans engaged in the French army under temporary contract.

In 1953 the missions to Na San, west of Hanoi, took up most of our time. The forces there had been digging in since autumn 1952, when the commanders had decided to transform it into a solid support base to stop the Vietminh's progress toward Laos, somewhat akin to what was attempted the following year at Dien Bien Phu. Situated in a mountainous region on T'ai land, the position could only be reached by air. Many civilian aircraft from Autrex, Aigle Azur, Cati, and Air Vietnam had been requisitioned to bring troop reinforcements and evacuate casualties. When we arrived we would go to the surgical area where the wounded were gathered to wait for their flight. Doctor (Captain) Clastres was in charge, assisted by two military nurses who instructed us in the care we were to administer during the flight. On the military craft that were not pressurized, it was particularly crucial to give oxygen to the wounded and to sustain their blood pressure.

One day, after a serious battle, we were warned to expect many casualties. When I landed on the field at Na San, two Dakotas carrying two of my fellow flight nurses were already on their way back to Hanoi with the first group of men. When the ambulances I was awaiting appeared at last, night was falling, the ceiling was very low, and the plane could no longer take off. So I spent the night helping the nurses prolong the "disconnections," intravenous injections of phenergan dolosal, a process that had been perfected by Doctor Henri Laborit to reduce the effect of shock from the injuries. I also assisted in an operation. That night I had a foretaste of what I would experience, though far more dramatically, ten months later in Dien Bien Phu.

I was able to admire the competence and the devotion of these two nurses. One hour after their arrival at the base, the wounded were "disconnected," treated, and ready to board the plane. These nurses were terrific young women. Since they were somewhat isolated among thousands of combatants, they were delighted to see us arrive. Our presence reassured them of the fate of their patients, once those had been settled on board. At the time there were still women in the surgical units. Later it was judged too dangerous. In Dien Bien Phu, after the first attacks, all French feminine presence would be forbidden.

On Ascension Day, just as the Mass I had attended was ending, a tiny plane, a Morane, brought in a Vietnamese soldier who had stepped on a mine during the conflict. His arterial tension was at four, his right leg was crushed, and his left leg was broken, as was his left arm. All day we fought to raise his blood pressure. As we were about to take off, his arterial tension had only risen to six. The pilot obtained permission to delay the flight. At 10:00 PM we placed the wounded man on board, disconnected and hibernated, with a transfusion of plasma. He survived the flight, but when I went to see him in the hospital in Hanoi, he had lost both legs and his left hand. It was heartbreaking.

The following day I flew to Xieng Khouang to fetch fourteen wounded, six badly. It was a stressful period. We were flying two missions a day. After Xieng Khouang, it was Luang Prabang. On my return to Hanoi I scribbled a few quick lines to my mother: "Barely back from Luang Prabang, I leave in a few minutes for Na San." I just had time to go by Lanessan Hospital, where I learned that the soldier who had lost both legs had died. Perhaps it was better this way. Had he survived, how would this young Vietnamese man have managed in the rice fields with wooden legs? At that time in Indochina, they were not yet using real prostheses, just simple pegs of wood.

The last weeks of June 1953 were calmer. Having flown down to Saigon with twenty-four severely wounded men, I was able to stay there for two days to relax with friends. The life I had been leading for the last two months thrilled me, and I was lucky to have an iron constitution, but days of rest were welcome to help me regain my strength.

In early July the rainy season flooded Hanoi. One went out barefoot in water that sometimes reached one's knees. One Sunday I was designated to represent the flight nurses on the airfield of Doson, near Haiphong, at a Mass celebrated for the dead of the Franche-Comté, one of the four groups of the Air Transport Command. The group commandant flew me over Ha Long Bay, a magnificent sight with its peaks surging out of the South China Sea, to which the mist gave an unreal quality. On the way back to Saigon in a Dakota carrying twenty-four more wounded destined for Grall Hospital, I had the good luck to go by Nha Trang on the north-eastern coast, not far from Dalat, and to discover its magnificent beach, lined with coconut trees and filaos and surrounded by mountains.

Back in Hanoi I was on my way up to Bach Mai to catch the first plane for Na San when our jeep was stopped on the edge of the trail. Operation Hirondelle was starting. I had a front-row seat to watch the launching, every three minutes, of the Dakotas that took off to parachute two thousand combatants over Lang Son on the Chinese border, and five hundred over Loch Binh, on a mission to destroy the Vietminh depots: their weapons, munitions, fuel, and so on. One of the Dakotas was unable to take off and crashed on the field. The pilot, who survived, found out that an additional load of supplies had been placed in his plane's tail compartment. The aircraft behind him was already rolling and I saw it lift off, avoid the obstacle, touch the ground again, and pull into the air in an incredible maneuver.

The evacuations from the different military operation theaters in Tonkin to Lanessan Hospital in Hanoi were short flights. But, regularly, evacuations were diverted from Hanoi to Saigon on Dakotas transformed into medical transports with twenty-four stretchers for the wounded. One reason was to ease the pressure on the hospital in Hanoi, which became quickly overwhelmed when large battles occurred. The day before such an event, we would go to Lanessan to see the wounded and get our orders, walking under the covered galleries that crossed the gardens and led to the different services. We often transported men wounded in the head, since the hospital specialized to treat them was the Grall Hospital in Saigon. On those occasions the flight could not go over the Annamitique chain of mountains, which reaches 2,600 meters, so the pilot had to follow the shore to avoid climbing that high. The flights were then seven hours long, with the risk of turbulence at low altitude. During that time we never stopped. We needed to watch the IVs, which would lose their rhythm at every variation in atmospheric pressure, as well as monitor the blood pressures, the pulses, and the respiratory rhythms. On those trips we were assisted by a male nurse from the air force health services. When we landed in Saigon, headquarters of the southern detachment, we would stay a few days, waiting for another flight nurse to arrive from the North, and we would effect, when ordered, evacuations from Seno, Vientiane, or Phnom Penh toward Saigon.

INTERLUDE IN NORTH AFRICA

In September 1953, after three intense months in Indochina, I was transferred to Algiers for two months to fly on the Junkers that secured the "Saharan lines." Oh, joy! I went with Alberte, one of my two cotrainees. For those two months we would fly separately during the week, but we would meet between missions. For hours in the evening we would exchange our impressions, and as soon as we had a free moment, we traveled as much as possible to discover Algeria, still very peaceful at that time.

From Maison-Blanche, the military base where we were posted, we would make a "Saharan circuit" that took us in the southern regions of Tunisia, Algeria, or Morocco. How can I describe the wonderment I felt on these journeys? The countryside I saw from the plane's windows had a beauty that took my breath away. I loved the contrast between the light-colored sand dunes and the bright green of the oases. The light was so beautiful, the clearness of the air so dazzling.

We flew in Junkers of the Algeria group, which secured the transport of passengers and food to the edge of the desert. Our cargoes looked like an unbelievable bazaar, piled up with passengers, mothers and babies, goats and kids, strong smelling fruits and vegetables, camel saddles, and Touareg musical instruments. Natives often mingled with soldiers and their families, and a few French or foreign tourists, especially in the Hoggar region, and even sometimes a few missionaries inspired by the personality of Father Charles de Foucauld.

Since those military planes were not pressurized, the heat and the bumps from flying at low altitude were very hard on the passengers. To tell the truth, the flight nurses did not do so well either, but we had to overcome our own malaise to help the mothers and the children who completely panicked at the slightest air pocket.

Navigation was rarely easy either. Sandstorms often affected the instruments. During a flight toward Ghardaia, an oasis in the north of the Algerian Sahara, the pilot was navigating blindly following a road until he saw a field where he could land. To the men who were bringing the landing steps to the plane, I heard him ask, "We're in Ghardaia, right?" The answer left him dumbfounded: We were in Biskra, three hundred kilometers northeast of our destination, at the foot of the Aurès high plateau.

We would land in stations with Indigenous Affairs offices, where we had friendly relations with the Saharan officers and their wives. The latter would ask us to make small purchases in Algiers, and we represented for them a bridge between the desert and civilization. I particularly remember a stop at In Salah, where the wives had asked us to get them a few sewing notions. We sensed their isolation—and their pleasure in our visit.

In these stations we met the famous Meharist officers who reigned, in the true sense of the word, on enormous sections of sand more vast than the territory of France. In Fort Polignac the captain des Illouzes had the bearing of a warrior-monk. All of them, with their proud traditions and their limitless sense of hospitality, carried themselves like true lords of the desert.

I still recall the cordial welcome offered us in Djanet by one of the officers who commanded the region in Tassili. We slept in a fortified village perched on a hill. The weather was hot, and I appreciated the rustic shower fabricated from a large tin can that would tip when its rope was pulled. Our host had lived thirty years in this lovely oasis lost in the mountains. He had just received his transfer orders to Germany and we were to bring him back to France. I have often wondered if this old desert rat was able to readjust to the European world.

On that same return flight I had to evacuate a sick woman suffering from nervous attacks, one who had caused me a few problems at our first landing. I was able to visit her later in the hospital in order to bring news of her to her family.

Our stay in Algeria did include some moments of relaxation, which Alberte and I used to rest on the beach or to visit cousins or to play tourist. We would climb into the high plateau of Djurjura, not far from Algiers, where the summit reached 23,000 meters, drive by bus to Cherchell, then return via the splendid Corniche road, which passes through Tipasa. There we would wander through the ruins of this ancient Roman city and admire its vestiges: amphitheater, temple, theater, large basilica, and Christian cemeteries.

But, finally, it was the missions that gave me the best occasions to cross the area in all directions and to discover the cities and oases lost in a desert of sand: Ouargla, Fort Flatters, Fort Polignac, Tamanrasset, Biskra, Aoulef, Adrar, Colomb-Béchar, Oran. I impatiently looked forward to discovering El-Golea, the Pearl of the Oases. But I was somewhat disappointed by the site. The influx of tourists arriving as early as winter to admire the sand roses robbed it of the charm that distance and the solitude of the desert can bring.

Everywhere we went we were warmly welcomed. In Tamarrasset the doctor drove me around the area in his jeep, and there I met Brother Jean-Marie, as well as the young and charming Little Sisters of Father de Foucauld. Unfortunately our stop was too short to allow us to visit Foucauld's hermitage in Assekrem. I regretted that, since I had always been impressed by the personality of this priest who had gone alone into the desert to live and pray among the nomads. Happily, many years later, I realized my dream by spending two weeks in the Hoggar with my husband and some friends. We slept under the stars, under the immense sky, near the small chapel where one of the brothers had celebrated the Eucharist for us. Then we hiked several days in the sumptuous scenery of the plateau, whose colors changed at dawn and at twilight, savoring the silence. It was easy to understand why the hermit of the Sahara loved the desert and felt closer to God there.

Certain missions took us into the south of Morocco and Tunisia. Every detail of every one of those flights has remained engraved on my memory. Among the passengers I had to attend to were two women and four children between age one and seven who were almost all airsick. There was also a seventy-three-year-old Arab woman who did not speak a word of French. With irresistible kindness she would force on me cakes, fruits, and drinks that I did not really want. Once I had made sure she had landed safely at one of our stops in Ghadames, I recovered from all these sweets by wandering in the old town, escorted by its administrator and a young second lieutenant.

Of the places I went, the one that left the deepest impression was Ghat, a pretty oasis dominated by the ruins of an old fort against a backdrop of enormous rocky cliffs in the distance. Near the vast central square, surrounded by houses almost red in color, women were playing the *tobal*, a sort of tambourine, to celebrate the return from Mecca of an Arab chieftain who also held the post of prefect. At twilight the palm trees became black cutouts on a scarlet sky. This vision accentuated further the character of the small town, built with true care for urbanism and with a surprising unity of style, despite being a mix of Arab and Sudanese architecture. As to the magnificent hospital in Ghat, many of our French cities might, at that period of time, have envied it.

My assignment in Algeria was nearing its end. With some nostalgia, I decided to take my leave of this country I had so loved by climbing to Notre-Dame of Algiers, from which I could view the splendid panorama over the bay, encircled by white houses. In fact, it was on taking off, just as in landing, that I most admired the view of this appealing town, so appropriately named the White City of Algiers.

Chapter Three

INTO THE MAELSTROM

While I was in North Africa beginning in September 1953, the situation in Indochina was evolving at an astonishing speed and was taking a decisive turn. On November 19, 1953, General Henri Navarre, who had replaced General Salan in May as commander in chief in Indochina, launched Operation Castor. Its goal was to concentrate totally on the site of Dien Bien Phu, one of the chief villages of the T'ai district, close to the Laotian border. The objective of the mission was to protect Laos, the first country to join the French Union, and to prevent a later advance by the Vietminh toward the west into that region, which held an enormous reserve of rice. Dien Bien Phu (Muong Theng in T'ai) was chosen for the establishment of this reinforced camp, primarily because an old landing strip there could be restored.

In the very heart of the T'ai mountains, the site consisted of a valley eighteen kilometers long and seven kilometers wide, carpeted with green rice fields. From north to south a river, the Nam Youm, a small branch of the Mekong River, flowed between relatively steep banks. For the French this place, surrounded by hostile, dark summits and a thick jungle, was all but inaccessible by road. But the landing strip would soon be repaired and made "Dakotable." Indeed the C47 would be indispensable to establish an aerial bridge with Hanoi, to bring the supplies necessary for the establishment of the camp, to ensure its resupply, and eventually to evacuate the wounded. Unfortunately, the location of Dien Bien Phu, three hundred kilometers west of Hanoi, stretched the limits of the plane's range. This would prove to be a major handicap.

On November 20 the first three battalions of paratroopers—those of Major Bigeard, Major Bréchignac, and Major Souquet—and a company of "French 75" guns were sent to Dien Bien Phu, followed on November 21 and 22 by three other battalions. Within three days, 4,445 men and 203 tons of material had arrived by air, flown in by 250 relays of Dakotas. Immediately the men got to work; everywhere people were digging, moving in, reinforcing, and creating underground shelters. Soon positions would be established and christened, curiously, with feminine names: Gabrielle, Anne-Marie, and Béatrice to the north; Dominique and Éliane to the east; Huguette, Françoise, Claudine, and Juno to the west; and, finally, Isabelle, quite separate from the others, at five kilometers south of headquarters. A surgical unit was set up, easy to locate by the few ambulances parked nearby.

On January 12, 1954, I returned to Indochina for the second time. This time my assignment was for six months, as the course of events in Tonkin had accelerated the need. In the North the team of flight nurses had been enlarged and the length of their stay had been extended.

When I first arrived by plane in DBP, the camp appeared to me already completely denuded. From the air it was a universe of tunnels, trenches, and shelters whose entrances were revealed and reinforced by logs and sandbags. Machine-gun posts were spotted on the hillsides, and on the plain, as we descended to land, I could see the brown tarps that still covered the shelters. Once I landed, the hills, green and wooded, seemed suddenly less hostile than the vast jungle universe we had flown over with its menacing density. In the distance a few rice fields still quivered in the wind, but the camp was closed in by a threatening jungle where paths must be carved out by machete.

In fact, since November 1953 DBP had become the main mission of the flight nurses stationed in Hanoi. Each day two of us were assigned to go into the remote camp and evacuate the wounded, whose numbers increased when the battalions effected a sortie to prevent encirclement by the enemy. The flight nurses waited either for an emergency flight, if a soldier was grievously wounded, or for a regular flight in the late morning or late afternoon, for casualties who had already received emergency care at the surgical unit. There were also victims of typhus, dysentery, and malaria.

Aware of the seriousness of the stakes, General Navarre, who had not obtained the means required for the execution of his plan, continued to request additional forces and supplies—which he never totally received. In France the governments of the Fourth Republic followed one after another, and Indochina, on the other side of the world from the French capital, did not weigh heavily with the electorate. René Coty had just been elected to the presidency of the Republic. The Communists, supported by the Marxist intelligencia, continued to pursue their course of sabotage and their campaign of disparagement of the war in Indochina, and Boris Vian and Harold Berg composed the song "The Deserter": "Don't go to war / refuse to go."

At the start of 1954 the Berlin Conference brought together representatives from France, the United States, Great Britain, and the Soviet Union to discuss the war. The forces of General Giap had already invaded the zone around Dien Bien Phu, but the commander in chief of the Vietminh troops abandoned his plan to attack, feeling that he did not yet have sufficient power. However, when the conference, attended by the foreign ministers of the four Great Powers—Georges Bidault, John Foster Dulles, Anthony Eden, and Vyacheslav Molotov—concluded with the announcement of a new peace conference in Geneva in May, China suddenly decided to bring massive support to the Vietminh so that the latter could arrive at the negotiation table with a strong position. China's covert support consisted of guns, antiaircraft weapons, munitions, trucks, and military instructors. In a very short time, the Vietminh combatants, in a monumental effort, brought artillery pieces into the Dien Bien Phu area, where they were concealed in tunnels. They dug trenches and encircled all the French positions. Suddenly the parameters of the conflict were completely changed, and the discovery of the power of the Vietminh artillery took the tacticians in the camp by surprise.

But Dien Bien Phu was not our only mission in the North. Often I flew to retrieve the wounded in Laos, in Xieng Khouang, in Luang Prabang, in Muong Sai, or in the Tonkinese delta, where conflicts were frequent and violent. These short evacuations were sometimes exhausting, and we often were the targets of antiaircraft fire. On February 8, as I found myself on alert at the villa where we were housed because our team leader, Renée Martin—called Martine—discovered I had been flying too much, I was called for a surgical emergency. Seven times in a row, with the help of a male nurse, I landed in Nam Dinh to load twenty-four wounded men lying on stretchers. We had to unload them twenty minutes later in Hanoi, all the while attentively watching over those who were oppressed by the rapid changes in altitude.

On February 28, 1954, just before I landed in Dien Bien Phu as I had so often before, a serious accident occurred. Two Bearcat fighter planes collided on landing; one of the pilots was killed instantly, the other was in a coma with a skull fracture. Usually men with head wounds were brought back to Hanoi and later evacuated to the Saigon hospital when their condition had stabilized. That day Doctor (Major) Paul Grauwin believed that the only chance to save the young pilot was to fly directly to Saigon.

I shall never forget this evacuation, which lasted five hours, with this sole patient on board. It left an indelible impression on each of us. The crew and the chief pilot, Captain Cornu, were all marked forever. The life of the young pilot was hanging by a thread and I was holding it in my hands. Two IVs dripped necessary blood and plasma into the veins of the injured young man. The changes in altitude were continually interfering with their functions, and I constantly had to adjust their flow. I also proceeded with a disconnection, took his pulse and gave him oxygen when it was called for, took his blood pressure, and injected heart tonics. I had only one patient, but I never worked so hard as during that trip. From time to time a crew member cracked open the door to inquire on the state of the patient. The atmosphere was heavy and anxious; it was night and cold, but pearls of sweat formed on my brow. When he arrived at the hospital, the pilot was still alive, but the struggle was not yet won. The next morning, before returning to Hanoi, I called the hospital for news; they told me his condition was stable. Sadly, ten days later he died without having regained consciousness. I felt an infinite sadness as I thought of his family.

Two days later I left Hanoi for the South, assigned alone to Nha Trang for two weeks. My mission was to evacuate the wounded of Operation Atlante, launched on January 20. Every day I flew to pick them up in Tuy Hoa, where they had been brought by ambulance or helicopter from all over the region of Qui Nhon, and brought them back to Nha Trang, sometimes to Saigon. More often than not, before landing in Tuy Hoa to pick up the wounded, the plane, to avoid flying empty, would parachute men or supplies. I observed with admiration this perfectly synchronized ballet of men jumping, one after the other, on signal. The drop of supplies, particularly of rice, was somewhat more acrobatic: The plane descended very low to drop its loads without parachutes then ascended with full power. But these low-altitude flights allowed me to enjoy the sight of these mountainous regions, where one suddenly dove toward the hollow of valleys surrounded by peaks. This tourist's view relaxed me before I returned to my role of flight nurse.

On March 13, in the officers' mess of Nha Trang, I was quietly using one of my few free moments to hang curtains in the room assigned to the nurses when I learned of the terrible attack launched by the Vietminh on Dien Bien Phu. My comrades, Renée Martin and Jaic Domergue, were assigned that day to retrieve the wounded from the camp. Even as the enemy artillery was firing with incredible violence, they managed, miraculously, to take off from Dien Bien Phu and bring back to Hanoi eight injured soldiers in one plane, nineteen in the other. But hell had only started.

At 5:15 PM several planes were destroyed on the ground before they could take off: one Dakota, one civilian Curtis, one C-119 Fairchild Packett, and two fighters—Bearcats. It was the first attack of this dimension, and it was directed on command post (CP) Béatrice, three kilometers northwest of the central position. The commander of the post and his adjutant were killed during the opening artillery fire, terribly intense. Each supporting position fought fiercely, but the Vietminh attackers, already only a few meters from the French positions in the trenches they dug, were ten times greater in number and sent their sappers ahead. In a few hours the shelters exploded under enemy fire. By early morning there remained practically no able-bodied officer.

While Béatrice was defending itself heroically, a shell landed in the middle of the central position, very close to the CP of the commander of Dien Bien Phu, Colonel Christian de Castries. It fell on the shelter of Lieutenant Colonel Jules Gaucher, whose chest was ripped open and limbs torn apart. He died in the arms of Father Heinrich, one of the four chaplains. His death was cruelly felt. The French Foreign Legion and the defense of DBP lost with him a prestigious leader. Grauwin called out urgently for ten liters of blood and a new surgical unit, which was assigned on March 14 to Isabelle. Around 6:00 PM an enemy artillery barrage started against Gabrielle. After the deluge of shells and the ground assault, the Legion was outnumbered eight to one and the post fell into enemy hands despite the French counterattack. The counterattack could only rescue the survivors of a regiment of Algerian sharpshooters who had fought all night. Major Roland de Mecquenem was taken prisoner, and his assistant, battalion commander Kah, had his leg torn off. He died at the hands of the Vietminh on March 27.

When the hills were lost to the enemy, the morale of certain officers began to drop severely. At dawn on March 15, Colonel Piroth, the artillery commander, committed suicide, feeling responsible for the failure of the French artillery to defeat the attack. Lieutenant Colonel Keller, chief of staff of Colonel de Castries, had a nervous breakdown and was replaced by Lieutenant Colonel Ducruix. The collapse of the posts Béatrice then Gabrielle stunned the T'ai troops of the 3rd T'ai Battalion, who were defending Anne-Marie. Exposed to intense Vietminh propaganda broadcasts over loudspeakers, many of them deserted, abandoning that position.

On March 15 a new surgical unit under Doctor (Lieutenant) Jean Vidal was dropped by parachute into the central position on the bank of the Nam Youm to reinforce Grauwin's unit. The following day a landing of paratroopers under the command of Major Bigeard, who had just returned from an operation after the success of Castor, revived hope in the hearts of the troops, thanks to the reputation of the battalion and its leader.

The landing strip was damaged and the Dakotas could no longer land to evacuate the wounded, who were piling up in the shelters in the most uncomfortable conditions. As soon as the field was repaired, the convoy nurses in Hanoi climbed aboard the Dakotas, which also parachuted in troops and packages. These planes were ready to land later for medical evacuations if the fire of enemy mortars and antiaircraft was not too violent.

Jack Coudert, piloting a Dakota from the Franche-Comté group, recalled in his book *La Dernière Luciole* (The Last Firefly):

On March 16, we are flying back to Hanoi after having dropped Major Bigeard's men. The chief of operations who awaits us on the ground in Hanoi informs us that we are returning into the breach for a medical pickup in Dien Bien Phu. The latest news announces the rehabilitation of the field and the possibility of landing there. One flight nurse is on board. I prepare my approach. I am in my landing axis with four minutes to touchdown. Just then all hell breaks loose. The first mortar falls at my end of the field, on the right of the plane, forming an enormous mushroom of dirt. Explosion after explosion follows and sprays the strip, preventing any landing.

Meanwhile Doctor Le Damany had found room for the wounded in the shelters not taken over by the battle. The battalion medical corpsmen increased their medical facilities by requisitioning the messes and the resting areas for the troops, as there was no longer any rest to be had. But another drama occurred in the principal unit. A 120-mm mortar shell fell on the triage tent, and thirty-five of the wounded were killed. In the abdominal surgery shelter, a 105-mm shell killed seven out of the eleven who had already undergone surgery. The x-ray room was then dedicated for the storage of bandages and medicines, as the only x-ray machine had been destroyed. Our ignorance of the strength of the Vietminh artillery certainly played a major role in drama of Dien Bien Phu. Doctor Grauwin called on the engineers, and the company of Lieutenant Maury, with the help of Sergeant Buczek's pioneers of the 8th BPC (Bataillon Parachutiste de Choc, or Parachute Shock Battalion), started to repair and consolidate the shelters. Many of those wounded during the attacks that followed owed them their lives, even though their role remains unacknowledged. How often, then and later, Buczek came by the unit close to his to see if he was needed. But the problem of available shelter grew worse every day, and a way to evacuate the wounded had to be found, since, despite many attempts, only two planes had succeeded in landing since March 15.

One of my fellow flight nurses, Michele Lesueur, left Hanoi on March 17 on a plane piloted by Lieutenant de Ruffray. The aircraft, painted with a red cross, carried only boxes of medicine. Ruffray managed to land, but the Vietminh started firing as the unloading began. The injured, patiently waiting on the field, rushed to get aboard. As the rain of bullets became very dense, the pilot pushed a bell to warn the personnel in back that he was taking off because he could no longer remain under the intense shelling. Some of the injured who could not get in were hanging for a moment on the tail of the aircraft. It took off before anyone could settle the evacuees. It rose slowly, painfully. When Michele counted her charges, she found thirty-two of them, many piled together at the rear of the plane. Meanwhile, two other transports circling the basin had witnessed the difficulties of the first and were unable to land under the enemy's violent attacks.

It was a beautiful day, March 18, and the parachute drops continued, one after another, in the sky above Dien Bien Phu. The landing strip was still in good shape. Major Darde, his crew, and convoy nurse Aimée Calvel arrived over the site, their Dakota wearing a red cross on its fuselage. Their plane also carried Doctor (Captain) Lavendier, from Bach Mai base, who wanted to judge for himself the risks facing the evacuations of the wounded. Each passenger wore a bulletproof vest. The second the plane landed, the Vietminh artillery attacked with unheard-of violence and the Air Command Post ordered the aircraft to take off. The plane was already on the way when a mortar shell fell so close that a piece of shrapnel injured Lavendier despite his protective vest. Major Darde succeeded in tearing the plane off the field and returning to Hanoi, where he surveyed the damage: nineteen hits. The same day two Dakotas from the Franche-Comté transport group were hit in flight.

On March 19, parachutes were raining down on the isolated camp. Lieutenant Biswang, an excellent pilot, having received permission to land, flew out of the circle of parachutes and landed. Elisabeth Gras, the flight nurse, rapidly hurried the less severely wounded on board while a medical corpsman from the unit helped her install the stretchers. The enemy artillery had already opened fire and Biswang moved the plane. He barely saved it. A 105-mm mortar exploded on the very spot he had just left. He continued to move forward and took off in a rain of shells. He had orders to drop off the injured in Muong Sai and return a second time to Dien Bien Phu despite the extremely dangerous conditions. But in midflight Major Guérin, who directed the Air Command Post, ordered him to turn around and pick up the other Dakotas that were flying over the strip, ready to attempt a landing to evacuate the injured, but flight nurses Christine de Lestrade and Brigitte de Kergorlay had their hopes crushed as they quickly returned without patients to Hanoi. Lieutenant Biswang and Elisabeth Gras did not know that they had just lived through the last daytime medical evacuation.

That same day, coming from Nha Trang after completing my two-week assignment, I returned to Hanoi to take my place in the North, according to a previous work assignment. Before arriving in Hanoi, on the field of Tan Son Nhut, the Saigon airport, I had run into a buddy.

"Where are you going, Geneviève?" he asked me.

"I am going back up to Hanoi and I am delighted!"

"Don't seek glory," he responded, smiling knowingly. "She escapes those who seek her."

On that March 19 there were still four hundred men, wounded in the attacks of March 13, 14, and 15, to evacuate. Lieutenant Colonel Descaves, commander of Gia Lam base, proposed to land the planes at night. Eight C-47s were planned for the first night, and if all went well, they would each make two trips. The landing strip would be marked by three small lights, two pointing out the beginning and one the end of the field. "We will try to land by surprise," explained Descaves to me as we were flying toward DBP, "engines off, while another plane will be circling the basin so as to camouflage with its engines the sound of the landing aircraft."

Descaves, who had perfected these nocturnal landings, wanted to make the first one, but he was in Gia Lam while all the convoy nurses on alert were in Bach Mai, the other airport. Since the bases were in opposite directions, it was deemed easier to bring one nurse from Hanoi by car rather than to fly one from the field in Bach Mai. So the telephone rang in our villa about fifteen minutes after my return from Saigon. Michele Lesueur, who was on call, was there alone with me. She picked up the phone, took the message, then turned very gently toward me and said, "I've already landed once in Dien Bien Phu since the March 13 attack; if you would like, you can go."

I didn't need to hear it twice. I grabbed my medical bag and oxygen kit and tore off in a jeep to Gia Lam. When I arrived at the field, the aircraft's propellers were already turning. I climbed aboard and the plane took off immediately. During the flight Lieutenant Colonel Descaves held a short briefing on the method for loading the wounded. Each aircraft had to take nineteen injured, thirteen sitting and six lying down. On one side of the plane were the seats—metallic buckets—for those who could sit up. To spare every second the stretchers were set right on the floor until the plane had reached cruising altitude, and then they were raised onto their racks.

We arrived over Dien Bien Phu. The night was dark, and we hoped that with luck we could land without drawing attention. I thought of all the injured men who awaited their evacuation and I prayed to God that the attempt would succeed.

The landing on a north heading went well. The aircraft rolled with its engines cut, and as soon as it landed, ground personnel pushed it around so that it could take off quickly, heading south. The ambulances were already there and everything went calmly and smoothly. I had time to greet the medical corpsmen from the surgical unit, most of whom I knew well. I shall always remember the expression of joy on the face of the man who directed the embarkation when he saw me. In the darkness, the tired faces of his men, badly shaven, seemed to emerge from another world. I couldn't help feeling how lucky I was to be able to head back to Hanoi once my mission had been accomplished.

"That was close!" the wounded cried out, noisily celebrating their joy at being on board the plane. One of them had escaped death by miracle. Hit in the abdomen on March 13 and operated on by Doctor Grauwin in the surgical unit, he had been buried under the roof of the space where the abdomen patients were recovering when it collapsed under enemy mortar shells. There was general elation. I rejoiced inside. We could now resume the evacuations!

That night five Dakotas managed to transport one hundred wounded under the nose of the Vietminh. Unfortunately our ruse was discovered, and the last three planes had to turn back without landing. Over the next days the nighttime evacuations were stopped in order to lower the enemy's vigilance. During the day on March 22, helicopters evacuated a few wounded to Muong Sai, where a C-47 waited to return them to Hanoi, since the range of the Sikorskys did not allow them to fly round trip between Hanoi and Dien Bien Phu (approximately 650 kilometers). I was there, in Muong Sai, with the crew when we welcomed the first evacuees. Muong Sai was a small town southwest of Dien Bien Phu, in Laos, where the field, large enough to accommodate Dakotas, allowed us to transfer the injured. On March 23 a helicopter, hit by a mortar on takeoff, fell heavily on Isabelle and burst into flames. The pilot, Sergeant First Class Bartier, who had just flown his thousandth mission in Indochina and rescued 250 wounded, was pulled out of the cockpit. Second Lieutenant Gambiez, the son of General Gambiez, commander of the southern zone of the Tonkinese delta, was killed, cremated inside the fuselage by the flames.

In Muong Sai a plan for a massive evacuation by Sikorsky helicopters at night was taking shape. The aircraft of two units were gathered there, a squadron of the air force and a company of the army. The commanders of each unit flew the first run. But the aircraft did not have night vision instruments, and the mission was a catastrophe: A helicopter crashed into the side of a mountain. When we heard this we were all dismayed. After the death of Second Lieutenant Gambiez, daytime helicopter evacuations had been suspended, and this second crash put an end to all these flights, although they had rescued 101 injured from Dien Bien Phu.

Other attempts were made to land Dakotas at night, counting on the element of surprise. Each evening the flight schedules and the number of attempts changed. Sometimes it was the weather conditions that precluded any landings. On the evening of the twenty-second, Commander Rousselot and Yvonne Cozanet brought back twenty-two wounded after an acrobatic takeoff. During the night of March 23, the Dakota of Lieutenant Arbelet flew out from Gia Lam with Aimée Calvel aboard. At the nurse's villa the sound of the telephone awakened me in the middle of the night. I dashed to get it, since my room was the closest, and I learned that Arbelet and his mechanic had been injured and were being cared for in the Dien Bien Phu unit. The plane would not return that night. I went back to bed, shivering, thinking of Aimée left in that hell. Yet I don't remember having been frightened when I myself was later stuck in Dien Bien Phu.

For Aimée it was only a false alarm, but our emotional reaction was intense. I later learned that when Arbelet touched the ground, a Vietminh commando opened fire. As the assault heated up violently, Arbelet pushed the alarm button and started to lift off. At that moment he and his mechanic were hit inside the aircraft. The plane settled back and the two men were carried to the unit where Doctor Grauwin and Doctor Gindrey attended them. The mechanic, Master Sergeant Favrot, had both knees broken. By sheer luck the pilot was less seriously injured. He believed he could fly his plane back to Hanoi, but to be safe Captain Payen, who coordinated the fighter planes from the ground, decided to leave with him. In the early morning of March 24, before the mist cleared up, Aimée placed on the floor of the Dakota the stretcher on which Favrot was lying. Despite the hits it took, the plane seemed in shape to fly. Aimée later told me that she was concerned until the plane finally took off. She had been given orders to sit in the aircraft in crash position, folded into a ball, knees drawn up under her chin.

On that same day we learned that Captain Koenig's Dakota from the Béarn Transport Group had been hit by a projectile, doubtless a tracer round, in one of his gas tanks. The tank exploded. I knew the captain well. He had requested a three-month extension of duty so that he could take his leave during his children's vacation. What a tragedy.

The enemy antiaircraft became frighteningly accurate. On March 25 another Dakota from the Béarn, under the command of Captain Boeglin, was hit as it approached Dominique at four hundred feet. The right-hand engine caught on fire, and the pilot, Sergeant Gay, decided to land in Dien Bien Phu. But hit once again, he cut the other engine and crashed in the barbed wire at the edge of the camp's trenches and a minefield west of CP Huguette.

In Hanoi we were now on full battle alert. At such times everything happened very quickly and all personnel tried to measure up to their best. Each day the pilots completed two to three missions to Dien Bien Phu. On the bases the mechanics worked relentlessly, day and night, until some had to be transported, near collapse from exhaustion, to the emergency room at Lanessan Hospital.

Two more planes landed on the night of March 25. Captain Dartigues and Yvonne Cozanet arrived in the first and evacuated nineteen wounded. Major Martinet and Elisabeth Gras were on the second plane. Under heavy fire Elizabeth managed to embark six wounded, but from the crew shot down yesterday, only Sergeant Gay got aboard the Dakota.

Three landings were planned for the night of the twenty-sixth: Captain Bouguereau and Paule Bernard, Lieutenant Erhard and Brigitte de Kergorlay, and Major Louis de Saint-Marc and myself. Paule succeeded in evacuating nineteen wounded and brought on board the last three members of the Dakota crew that had crashed two days earlier. Brigitte could only take on nine men, as her plane had to take off quickly under the guns of the Vietminh.

I was aboard the third aircraft. Because of troubles with the radio, the ambulances were not yet at the landing strip when we arrived. The shelling intensified. Major de Saint-Marc considered it too risky to wait any longer because, as he later told me, one of his engines had shown signs of trouble on the way over. As the plane's engines began to turn, the ambulances approached. I could see them heading toward the plane. I rushed to the cockpit. Too late! The plane was already underway and immediately lifted off. I was crushed, and on the way back to Hanoi I could only think of those men who believed they were so close to freedom. I imagined their despair. I wanted at all cost to return and take them away.

Yvonne Cozanet, our team leader for the northern group, argued with me. She thought she would lead the next mission, but she at last accepted that I had to take her turn and I thanked her for it. Since my mission had not been completed, it was quite normal that I should be the one to go back.

But that same evening, aware of the danger that awaited me, I wrote a very long letter to my mother. I hoped that letter would help her understand that if I didn't return, I did not die for nothing. At least she would find, I hoped, in reading my words, a certain consolation, and perhaps some pride.

Chapter Four
THE TRAP CLOSES

On March 28 at 4:15 AM I was off again to Dien Bien Phu, where we arrived an hour and a half later. Visibility was very poor. Twice the pilot tried to find the landing field, and twice he took off again on discovering that he was not on the right axis. On the third attempt we landed between two small, dim lights that pointed to the start of the landing strip. But we drove slightly off the track and knocked over a picket of barbed wire. The pilot stopped the aircraft abreast of the ambulances and the wounded were settled on board. The French artillery guaranteed us some protection.

The mechanic went out to inspect the plane to verify that the barbed wire had not damaged the cabin and returned distressed; the oil reservoir had been pierced and was leaking. As to the oil pressure, it showed zero. There was no way we were going to be leaving.

This was terrible news to our patients, some of whom had come to the field twice, even three times, in hopes of being evacuated. This time they had believed their suffering would end.

We disembarked the men who were only lightly wounded and brought them and the crewmembers under shelter. The more severely wounded still needed to be unloaded, but the stretcher bearers were still waiting on the field for the ambulances. Luckily the mortar fire was scarce and distant. The ambulances finally arrived and brought all the casualties back to the main infirmary of GM 9 (Mobile Group 9), where the evacuees were gathered.

The aircraft was moved to the edge of the landing strip so that it wouldn't interfere with other landings. Hanoi would have to send a new part to repair the plane, but the major in charge of flights into Dien Bien Phu forbade any daytime repairs, finding the risks too high. I gathered my equipment, medical kit, oxygen pump, and blankets and went to the medical unit, where I found Doctor Grauwin and his team, who questioned me eagerly for news from Hanoi. They never thought we would be back so soon; only the day before they had received a letter from me.

It was still night, and the fog protected the plane and rendered it invisible to the Vietminh. Alas, it cleared around 10:00 AM, and their artillery went into action. At 10:30, on the fourth round, our aircraft was hit. With emotion we watched the flames and the smoke that enveloped it.

The day was calm, no one needed me at the unit, and I took the opportunity to visit a few friends. My eyes were still full of hallucinating visions of the nighttime evacuations I had been undertaking for the last ten days. I had difficulty getting an idea of the real state of affairs in Dien Bien Phu. I imagined it to be catastrophic. In fact, during those last days of March, one could still walk about the camp freely, though once in a while I heard a mortar explosion, so I scrupulously wore the helmet I was given.

My steps led me toward the 1st Foreign Legion Parachute Battalion, where I found the same atmosphere as before March 13. The brother of a former flight nurse was attached to this group, and cordial relations had been established between the paratroopers and the flight nurses, especially with the very popular Loulou Martin. Under a smile and an unflappable calm, Loulou, wounded on January 12 and again on March 5, hid an exceptional courage. I gave them news of two wounded comrades who had come by our villa in Hanoi a few hours earlier.

They also wanted to know how another comrade was faring. He had been evacuated the day before after receiving severe wounds in an action to liberate Huguette 6. Finding the battalion doctor overwhelmed with casualties, this lieutenant had walked toward the medical unit and, despite the injuries to his face and his chest, had managed on the way to help a Legionnaire who was having difficulty climbing aboard the tank that was to evacuate him. When he reached the unit, Doctor Grauwin discovered a large, gaping hole where his mouth had been. The skin of his chin and cheeks hung in shreds on his chest with fragments of teeth and bone. It was terrifying to see. Another surgeon, Doctor Gindrey, seeing him unable to breathe, performed a life-saving tracheotomy.

But his troubles were not over. When the pilot of the first of three Dakotas that landed that night gunned the engine because the enemy shells were getting closer to the aircraft, the flight nurse on board noticed that a casualty had been left behind in the GMC ambulance and put him on board—to his great relief, since he could not call out and was seeing with anguish that the plane was about to leave without him. Once aboard he drew the flight nurse's attention by showing her the tag around his neck, and then she recognized in this man, whose face was hidden behind an enormous bandage, a good friend from the Sahara. All the men in the 1st BEP (1st Foreign Legion Parachute Battalion) were happy to learn that the evacuation went well and that their comrade's life was not in danger.

They handed me letters already written; some promised to have theirs ready later that evening. At the time I trusted that I would leave that night in the next Dakota landing to evacuate the injured.

The officers welcomed me very warmly. Lieutenant Colonel Pierre Langlais, who commanded the 2nd Airborne Group, invited me to lunch. That evening I dined with Colonel Lemeunier, commander of the 13th Demi-Brigade of the Foreign Legion, who succeeded Colonel Gaucher, killed in his shelter March 13. At headquarters Major Guerin introduced me to Colonel de Castries, the commander of Dien Bien Phu.

Before me stood a man of medium size, rather thin and pale, with sharp features and an aquiline profile, "resembling a subject painted by el Greco," as the author Jules Roy described him in his book *The Battle of Dien Bien Phu*. In truth Colonel de Castries did not want to command a defensive base, but General Navarre had assured him that it would be on the offensive, and he had the courage to accept the command.

Colonel de Castries welcomed me very amicably and hoped that I could leave that evening with the wounded. I asked him if I could go over to Isabelle, where my cousin Louis de Chastenet had been since the desertion of the T'ai battalion from Anne-Marie. I knew through my family that his mother was very worried. But the road between Isabelle and Central Command, considered too deadly, had been closed. Captain Hervouët, who commanded the tanks at Dien Bien Phu, then charged Sergeant Ney to ask for news during the daily contact with Isabelle. The next day Ney reported: "Captain, Lieutenant Chastenet asked me to tell Geneviève that all is well and asked me to give her a kiss."

"Well, go ahead!" said the captain.

"Needless to say I didn't feel that brave," Ney later sheepishly admitted to me with a smile because he was excusing himself for having "stolen" this kiss, "but taking my courage in my hands, I left the block-house to go find Geneviève." The command to give me a kiss had evidently been added on his own.

That afternoon we went to pray on the grave of Dartigues' crew. A few hours after conveying nineteen casualties to Hanoi on March 26, as I noted earlier, Captain Dartigues had taken off again on a flight to drop paratroopers over Dien Bien Phu. His mission accomplished, his Dakota was hit by antiaircraft fire and crashed, killing seven people. That day the flight commander gave the order to stop all lower-altitude paratrooper drops to avoid further slaughter. This sad episode illustrates the daunting difficulties faced by the military air transports that flew in to the base two to three times a day. A lieutenant gave me the wedding rings and personal objects that had been recovered so that I could return them to the families of my lost comrades.

"A plane will be landing this evening around 9:00 PM," Major Guerin suddenly announced. Immediately I rushed over to the infirmary to see the wounded, and I begged Doctor Le Damany, who was in charge of evacuations, "We must absolutely first board those that we had to unload last night!" "Unfortunately I can't promise you that," he answered. "First priority goes to the urgent cases." I said goodbye to everyone and was taken to the landing field with the rest of the crew.

An ammunition depot near the parking area for the fighter planes had just been hit and enormous fireworks illuminated the sky. Our jeep flew by the depot at full speed just before a new explosion shot out flashes of light and sparks all around. The complete crew, sitting on the steps of the transit shelter, awaited the plane and, straining their ears, listened for the sound of an engine. Enemy fire forced us to retreat inside the shelter. The wounded to be taken aboard were still at the infirmary and would arrive by ambulance as soon as the plane began its steep descent.

The weather was very bad. Nine o'clock came, nothing. Nine-thirty, still no plane. We took the path back to quarters, this time detouring the depot. I was taken to 1st BEP, and there I spent my first night at Dien Bien Phu, a very calm night, on a stretcher between two male air force nurses. At that time I didn't have a feeling of being sealed in at Dien Bien Phu because each night one or two Dakotas were designated to go pick up the wounded in the entrenched camp.

After breakfast I walked over to headquarters to join up with Major Blanchet and the rest of the crew, who had spent the night among the commandos. Later, back at the surgery, I was teased over my failed departure: "It's obvious you really don't want to leave us!"

On that day I did not have to intervene as a nurse, but trying to make myself useful, I circulated throughout the central position, helmet on my head, and lowered myself into the trenches to distribute to the wounded the cigarettes, oranges, and concentrated milk sent by the Red Cross and Madame de Castries by parachute to Dien Bien Phu. I was not worried so much with the possibility of my return to Hanoi, but while the situation was getting worse and Vietminh shells were falling on the landing field, the possibility of a landing was becoming more and more risky.

On the evening of March 29 we exchanged new goodbyes. "I'll see you tomorrow," said Sioni, the driver of the jeep, smiling, believing we would not be leaving. And the next day it was I, smiling also, who went to see him. "Who was right?" said Sioni, mischievously.

Once more I went to GM 9 to visit the wounded, who were impatiently waiting for news, and I tried to cheer them up. "It will be tonight," I told them as I left. At this point there were 250 injured who need to be evacuated.

The plane's arrival was announced for 12:30 that night. I was picked up and driven again to the field. It was dark as ink and pouring rain. We got stuck in the mud, sliding about and slipping into the ditch and barbed wire fences. Abandoning the jeep, we proceeded on foot. I found it impossible to believe that a plane could land under such conditions; it would, I thought, be suicide. The driver tried to appear optimistic, but I had no illusions.

The plane appeared, piloted by Major Martinet, who commanded Group Béarn (whose second in command, Major Blanchet, was the pilot of our damaged plane). It was coming in on a nearly vertical path. I wanted to scream, "Don't let them land, it would be murder!" And indeed, that was somewhat the same thing Major Blanchet said to his boss on the radio. The strip was slippery, a veritable skating rink, and the first third of it was damaged. Major Guerin, from his air traffic control station on the ground at Dien Bien Phu, forbade Martinet to proceed with the landing. The trap was starting to close.

Once more I passed the night at 1st BEP with the medical corpsmen of the air force without the possibility of personal privacy, taking advantage of those rare moments when I found myself alone to take a quick wash. Outside, without protection against the bombardments, were the latrines.

On March 30 the wait for an evacuation that was becoming more and more improbable started to weigh on us all. As did the forced inactivity. I spent my day at the ward and had lunch with the medical team. Our meals were composed of canned goods such as corned beef, but some vegetables and mixed salads were sometimes parachuted in to us in packs. I have no recollection of taking meals at the surgical unit in those periods of intense work. There it was necessary just to grab whatever we could in a hurry—"eat and run." Later, during moments of calm, I was invited to eat with the paratroopers or legionnaires. Those meals were moments of real relaxation and great uplifting, when I could leave the surgical unit with its oppressive atmosphere, charged with offensive odors, and my pressing duties for a short time of frank comradery and an exchange of news, which I always brought back to my wounded. But events were soon to rush forward precipitously.

At four in the afternoon shells from mortars and 105-mm howitzers started to fall. By five the artillery fire had reached an unbelievable violence. Never, even on March 13, had Dien Bien Phu endured such concentrated bombardments. I felt as if it was the end of the world. The impacts shook our bunker. Pieces of earth fell from the roof and we wondered how long it would hold up. Nobody said a word. All around there were wounded men bearing their sufferings with courage, and I knew that at dawn, when the battle decreased, the stretcher bearers would bring the new wounded. How could I sleep in such circumstances?

To satisfy natural needs, men used tins. I couldn't do the same, and after several hours I had to go outside, under the shells, asking God to protect me. The shelling lasted all night; the din was terrifying. It was fortunate I was in the medical unit because it was now impossible to circulate in the camp, and soon two extra arms would be useful. The other members of my crew thought the same and went off to support the team of air force medics by carrying the injured.

By dawn on March 31 the unit was already full. The stretchers were placed on the ground, wherever there was room between the beds of the wounded already there. The corridor of the unit, a long tunnel, narrow, muddy, and barely lit, was immediately blocked with stretchers that one had to step over to get past. Outside on the rampart at the entry to the unit, men waited on their stretchers until room could be found to place them under shelter. Some of them received new wounds and others were killed at the door to the unit. It was utter hell. The sound of the artillery was deafening, and the wounds of the injured had dirt mixed in with their blood.

As the wounded were brought in, the PIMs (*prisonniers internés militaires*, "military prisoners") cleaned them up as much as they could. Doctor Grauwin had put me in charge of emergency care of the most seriously wounded. I worked under the light of an electric lamp in the corridor, one knee on the ground, the other on the edge of the stretcher. I had never been in such a situation, so dramatic, but confronted with wounded men, you only think to relieve their pain, and I was glad to succeed in doing the intravenous injections of phenergan dolosal, which helped quiet the wounded and allowed them to sleep.

How can I describe the uninterrupted flow of injured, the heartbreak at our inability to shelter all of them and to operate on them fast enough?

On the basis of his long experience, Grauwin conducted the triage, deciding who should be operated on first. This posed terrible choices, because an abdominal operation took as much time as five or six amputations, and he had to make his decision according to the most urgent cases. Gindrey was operating without a break, with or without Grauwin's assistance. With each explosion, the earth shook and debris fell from the ceiling of the operating room. Fortunately it was tented with parachutes, but the rain liquefied the soil and droplets sometimes fell on the operating table. Across the hall the recovery room, which held fifteen beds, was packed with the addition of fifteen stretchers on the ground. The wounded who were lightly injured were quickly attended to then returned to their units under a rain of mortar shells because we had no room for them.

That night, in less than an hour, the Vietminh took three of our positions, Dominique 1 and 2 and Éliane 1. Only Dominique 3 defended the road that led to our unit and the headquarters of Colonel de Castries. That night an event took place that would be retold many times. Lieutenant Brunbrouck, commanding the 4th Battery of 2/4 RAC, saw waves of Vietminh running toward him. He had received orders to pull back but had refused, and waiting until the last moment, he lowered his artillery for direct fire right in front of his position, mowing down the enemy columns. Without Brunbrouck, Dien Bien Phu may well have fallen that night, but at that moment I didn't understand how close the camp came to being overrun, and many of the combatants also were hopeful.

Early in the morning of March 31, a stretcher brought us Lieutenant Robert Chevalier from the Bigeard battalion. He had been shot in the head the previous afternoon during a counterattack. The bullet had severed his spinal cord and paralyzed him. When he arrived at our unit, in desperate condition, Doctor Grauwin's diagnosis was that we could do no more than to alleviate his pain. It was the most dramatic moment I can recall from those days.

The anguish of Robert Chevalier increased moment by moment. His paralysis progressed, first to his legs, then to his abdomen, his chest, and his arms. His breathing was more and more feeble. "Geneviève, promise me I won't die?" I turned my head without answering and felt desperately helpless. He was fighting death and I was in charge of giving him water in a small spoon, but he could barely swallow. I tried to numb his pain with shots of morphine and soften his anguish by staying by him whenever I could. The chaplain came to his bedside and deposited on his tongue a minute piece of the Host.

This was my first real contact with death since my father's death in 1934. I needed to tame its specter in the seemingly interminable face-off that was coming, whose outcome I already knew. Many of the wounded I had seen arrive at the unit were dying. With Robert Chevalier, it was a long journey toward the end; we waited together, and I could do nothing except ease his pain and be there with him. I kept thinking of his family, who must have received the impersonal and cryptic telegram sent to each family after the airlifts had stopped: "Impossible to write. All is going well."

I was by his side when Lieutenant Chevalier stopped breathing. It was a moment I shall never forget. Years later I had the opportunity to meet his sister in the southeast of France. That was a very moving moment, and she was deeply happy to be able to speak with the person who had been at her brother's side at the time of his death.

At night the wounded could no longer be brought in on stretchers because of the shelling, which left more time for those already at the unit. But the deafening sound of artillery fire never ceased. During those three days and nights at the end of March, the sense of our helpless inability to save all our wounded, or even to bring them all under shelter from the shelling, became intolerable. At times I just wanted to sleep, to sleep and not wake up to that awful reality. But sleep was out of the question; there was too much to do.

When the shelling finally calmed down, the Vietminh were close to the landing field. Planes could no longer land. The trap was now completely closed. For the injured that news was dramatic. For me it was different. I knew that I would be able to continue caring for my patients, that I would not have to abandon them. In fact, several times I feared that when the combat stopped (we had had several days of respite after the three-day attack in mid-March) no one would ask for my opinion and I would have to leave on the first plane that could land, since my role was that of flight nurse, not ground medic. I well knew that High Command no longer wanted women in Dien Bien Phu. On March 14 it had even sent back Colonel de Castries' secretary. But in the meantime I was happily stuck at the camp and had only one thing left to do: care for and stay with the wounded.

A certain calm having returned in early April, life found a new rhythm. Since evacuations were now impossible, the unit was transformed into a true small, subterranean hospital. Doctor Grauwin entrusted me with the care and oversight of forty men, the most vulnerable who came out from the recovery room. This sudden "promotion" took me by surprise. It was not so much my qualifications as the urgency of the moment that motivated it. In medical units each nurse had a role to play, but none gave long-term care since, usually, the wounded were evacuated to Hanoi.

Now the real adventure would start for me. It would test, morally as well as physically, in the most radical manner, whatever strengths I possessed at the dawn of my twenty-ninth year. But it also would give meaning to the rest of my life.

Chapter Five

AMONG THE WOUNDED

"Geneviève, when it's all over, I'll take you dancing!"
The eighteen-year-old man who proffered this gallant invitation stood by my side gazing at the desolate view of the battlefield of Dien Bien Phu: the once-verdant rice fields dusty and riddled with metal fragments, the peaks so dearly defended whose earth held only a vast cemetery, the dark hills where the Viet artillery lay in wait, and a tangle of trenches and barbed wire that transformed the plain into a gigantic spider web.

On this afternoon in April 1954, Haas, a young German Legionnaire, still displayed a morale of steel. Yet if he wanted to stand, he needed to lean the stump of his arm on my shoulder. A corporal in the 2nd BEP (2nd Foreign Legion Parachute Battalion), Haas had been wounded three weeks earlier. Horribly mutilated by shell fragments, both arms and one leg had to be amputated. To avoid the risk of infection, the stumps were left open. Each change of bandages caused him to howl in pain. To be eighteen in Dien Bien Phu . . . and a triple amputee for the rest of his life.

That day, during a calm in the battle, my young patient had expressed a desire to breathe some fresh air at the entrance of the surgical unit, which he had not left since his operation, and asked me to accompany him. So off we went down the long, dark tunnel, I supporting him as well as I could, trying not to cause him more pain, Haas hopping on his good leg and leaning on me. His will and his courage tore me up more than I could let myself show him. And through it all he still found the strength to make jokes. After the fall of Dien Bien Phu, I saw Haas in Paris at the reeducation center of the Invalides where he was fitted with prostheses. In fifty years of closely following my former patients, I rarely saw an amputee walk as well. And later, when he came to the reunions of Dien Bien Phu combatants, he was always the one with the most spirit.

Every casualty in my charge was confined, crowded in this strange underground hospital. At the center of the unit ran a long, narrow hallway opening on the right to the shelters for the wounded, where three metallic beds were superimposed on three levels. On the left a small corridor led to the operating room opposite the recovery room. At its end was the x-ray room. This hall started at the rampart that opened to the triage room, the kitchen, the sterilizing room, the refectory, and the dorm. All these installations were quite basic. To guarantee the asepticity of the operating room, the space was simply hung with parachute fabric. Yet despite all this, and the lack of equipment, the surgeons performed miracles every day.

Situated near Colonel de Castries' command post, the main medical unit was divided into two wings. One was directed by Doctor Grauwin, the other by Doctor Gindrey. Grauwin had been due to return to France but volunteered to stay to replace a sick surgeon who was leaving for two weeks of rest. An army doctor under temporary contract, Grauwin was about forty years old and was completing his second tour in Indochina. His experience, his calm, and his aplomb made him the man in charge. He knew how to be rough in training and how to open a bottle of wine in celebration. A heavy smoker, he had wide shoulders, physically and figuratively. His presence contributed positively to the morale of the injured, who trusted him totally. In charge of triage and the follow-up of the most grievously wounded, he operated less than Gindrey but was always there to advise or to take over a serious procedure if circumstances called for it.

Gindrey, in turn, was a young military surgeon, totally committed to his specialty. Working for hours at a time, he did not leave the bloc. Like Grauwin he worked bare-chested in the unit, in the heat heightened by the rays of the enormous lamp that illuminated the operating field. He was not talkative and did not show his feelings. When in April his young wife, a nurse in Saigon, lost the baby she was carrying, he continued to work as usual without giving in to his emotions.

Doctor Grauwin's team, to which I belonged, included individuals with diverse talents. The head nurse, Marant, was at once an anesthesiologist, a recovery specialist, an instrument nurse, and an x-ray assistant. Sergeant Deudon, who had completed three years of medical training, curiously held the two functions of surgical aide and dietician. Sergeant N'Diaye, a Senegalese, was in charge of pre- and post-operative care. Corporal Lachamp served as secretary, and Private First Class Perez assisted nurse Marant. Four African nurses assisted N'Diaye and Deudon. A fifth nurse, Chief Corporal Kabbour, was in charge of sterilization. Two North Africans drove the ambulances, and two Legionnaires, Sioni and Cortes, drove the jeeps attached to the medical unit. Sioni also gave me precious help carrying my equipment and assisting with the heavy bandaging. Finally, Julot Vandamme, from communications, was a one-man orchestra, holding the varied roles of telephone operator, switchboard operator, orderly, and person responsible for the electric system.

Gindrey's team was composed of head nurse Levasseur, surgical assistant Bacus, instrument and recovery nurse Corporal Bescond, and four Vietnamese nurses, Hoat, Thanh, Bong, and Khanh. They all did their jobs with great dedication and competence.

In this underground of suffering, every day I attended to the wounded, giving shots, changing bandages, and distributing medicine. But that was not a reason to forget about their diet. At my request Deudon prepared a tasty soup with the fresh vegetables that were parachuted down to us. Of course it tasted somewhat the same every day, but it was easier for the injured to digest and certainly easier to swallow than the military rations that were our daily lot. Sioni also helped me to distribute the soup.

Very soon I realized the importance of a woman in the midst of battle. When wounded, the toughest man becomes as vulnerable as a child and needs to feel supported. "Nothing and no one," wrote Doctor Grauwin in his memoir *J'étais Médecin à Dien Bien Phu*, "can replace a young woman at the bedside of an injured soldier—not only at the rear hospitals but especially at the front, because of all this gentleness, this patience, this mysterious femininity that comes through in the most mechanical and most professional care."

In Dien Bien Phu I was in a way a mother, a sister, a friend. "You were, for many of us, a small piece of our native land, where the woman lived who waited for us, over there on the other side of the world," Chief Sergeant Fantinel would write me years later. "Thank you, dear Geneviève, for having given us your care, your soul, and a fragment of dream." Three times he was wounded and three times he was cared for at the unit.

My mere presence, because I was a woman, seemed to render this hell a little less inhuman. "If she had not been there," Serge Genty later told his wife, "I could not have gotten through it." This is not because it was I. Others would have played the same role in my place. But I had the luck to hold that role and it illuminated the rest of my life. How could I not melt with emotion when Courtiade, a paraplegic, told me, "Every time you walk into my room my morale goes up 100 percent." One day he called me in, triumphant: "Look, Geneviève, I can move my toe!" Every day I made a point to check his progress and encourage him to pursue his efforts.

Simon Marie was nineteen. He had been hit by a grenade as he was coming out of a tunnel. "When it exploded, I did not feel a thing," he said, as reported to his commander. "I was covered in earth and I could feel I was losing my blood. I shouted out; I believe I called for my mother. Besides my eyes having burst, my hands were also a mess." Simon did not know yet that he had lost his sight and that he would lose several fingers on each hand to amputation. Taken to a first-aid station, then by ambulance to the surgical unit, he stayed in the recovery room until the fall of Dien Bien Phu because the doctors did not want him to feel alone or abandoned. His face was covered in bandages, his hands were wrapped like a mummy's. "One month and a half in a hole, with two meters of dirt between you and the sky, is a long time," he said. "We were already prisoners before the time came."

As often as I could I came by to slip him an encouraging word, to bring him a drink or a cigarette that I lit for him. Soon the blinded youth, whose morale remained excellent, started spreading a little laughter around him. When his condition stabilized he tried with his poor mutilated hands to play the harmonica—and he succeeded, to the great joy of his comrades. His morale failed only once, after the fall of the base. The Vietminh had taken all the bandages and all the medicines. I heard him murmur, "What's happening? No one is taking care of us." I had to explain to him what was going on.

As I write these words, tears come to my eyes because the affection that connected me to these men, the affection that continues to connect me to them, shall never fade. It is an affection mixed with admiration because they "held up" in these underground bowels—humid, hot, and foul smelling—and that is proof of rare courage. What can I say then about this blind youth of nineteen who not only kept up his morale but also brought some cheer to the recovery room? After his liberation, a year in hospital, and twenty operations, Simon Marie settled in the Aveyron, where he fabricated models under the admiring eyes of the village children. One day when I telephoned, he explained that he had very sophisticated tools to help him do his work but that from time to time blood would spurt from his damaged fingers.

These memories continue to haunt my dreams and my nights every time I have to talk about them. They carry a part of hell with them, and yet I always manage to find in them a glimmer of light. When a little harmonica tune plays in my head, I can only think of the tenderness in the eyes of those men whose pain I tried to lessen.

Among the men wounded in the abdomen, who all had artificial anuses because of their injuries, one in particular worried me: Lieutenant Rondeau from the 5th Battalion of Vietnamese paratroopers. Injured on the day of my arrival in Dien Bien Phu on March 28, he was one of the first casualties who could not be evacuated. I can still see him, suffering from an infected salivary gland, with a fever of 105 degrees, delirious and wandering down the central hall clothed only in the bandages that cover his abdomen and his ears.

After a few days of antibiotic treatments, he recovered, but his morale was low and he often asked for me. Another time he stood again at the door of Death, and I felt in his glance a profound sadness. Yet every time he pulled himself up and, forgetting his own misery, wanted to show us his gratitude. He was an artist: The Madonna with Child he drew at Easter for Doctor Grauwin with an ordinary pencil, a little Mercurochrome, and some methylene blue, looked strangely like a Matisse. He copied the same image for Father Heinrich, framed in an oval that evoked an Easter egg. On the first of May, he offered me a lily of the valley made of a wire, some cotton, and leaves from the green paper that protects the compresses. These are gifts one can never forget.

Rondeau was to be one of the rare officers released by the Vietminh. It seemed his ordeal was nearing its end, but following a medical complication, he died a few days after his liberation.

During the course of that night of horror, March 30 to 31, our beloved 1st BEP, with which the flight nurses had forged many friendships, paid dearly. Fournier and Boisbouvier arrived at the unit, but once their wounds were bandaged they went back into combat. For Lieutenant Rolin, it was different: Shot in the leg, then hit by a grenade fragment as he was climbing to the assault at Éliane 2, he was treated by a medic and pulled into a shelter where he spent the night. At dawn he was brought into the surgical unit where Grauwin hesitated whether to operate or amputate. Finally he handed him over to Gindrey for an operation. Later Rolin was placed in a room just across the corridor from the operating room, where he remained until May 10. He was completely silent and I never heard him complain. He was so exhausted that he could not read or do anything to occupy those long days. Luckily, there were people milling around him and visits from his mates from the 1st BEP.

For three weeks in the evenings I was able to watch over my patients in this unit since that was where, when my work was done, I opened a stretcher between two beds for a short rest during the calm moments. To tell the truth I did not sleep well, for those dramatic days from March 30 to April 2 haunted me. Sleepless nights succeeded one another, and, wanting me to recuperate, Doctor Grauwin offered me a sleeping pill. I had never before taken one and the result was catastrophic. I spent the night in a sort of nightmare, feeling that my bed was collapsing under me. But at least, since the fighting had calmed down, we could go occasionally to the opening of the tunnel and breathe some fresh air. When I answered the calls of nature I no longer risked being found wounded or dead in an embarrassing position.

Among the men wounded in the abdomen was a Mauritian, Niang Abdoul Moktar from the 4th Regiment of Colonial Artillery, injured in the course of the conflict in which the artillery played such a major role. Like Rondeau he had an artificial anus and required daily nursing. From that time on he expressed to Doctor Grauwin and me a deep devotion. Every year he sends me holiday wishes written in very fine French by a Mauritanian scribe. For the fortieth anniversary of the end of the fighting at Dien Bien Phu, our association offered him a trip to France. It was the first time I had seen him since those days and we were both very moved. How handsome he was in his turban and *gandoura*, a tunic of wool or cotton under a burnoose, which was the hooded wool cloak worn by the Arab troops.

In the unit reserved for the amputees were Phuc and Huan, with the faces of children. Among the injured Vietnamese, I still stay in touch with two of them. Tran The Ty, with both legs amputated, was hit on April 7 when his battalion, the 5th Vietnamese Parachute Battalion, came to the support of Éliane 2. Nguyen Van Nhon of the 6th Parachute Battalion was wounded twice and his leg was amputated in Dalat after his liberation. They were both silent and never uttered a complaint. At their liberation by the Vietminh they were assigned to a sordid camp in Saigon, where I went to visit them in 1955 with Doctor Grauwin.

How could I ever forget Serge Genty, serving in Bigeard's battalion, so young and so courageous? On April 10, during the recapture of Éliane 1, he was wounded by shrapnel and a grenade that hit him in the belly, the feet, and the back. He had to be catheterized to supplant his severed urethra. Though it was very painful for him, he did not complain. After the fall of the base, deprived of care, he suffered cystitis that caused him terrible pain. Fortunately he was liberated on May 19, and I was able to see him at Lanessan Hospital after my own release. His weight had fallen to thirty kilos. Later I ran into him at Val-de-Grâce. He had undergone fifteen operations before returning home—which did not prevent him from going to war in Algeria in February 1955.

Corporal Michel Chanteux lay wounded in the same shelter as Serge. Dropped by parachute for the second time, he had been wounded in the arm, then in the head during food drop missions, but returned to the fight. The third time, during an assault, a Vietminh soldier opened his abdomen with a bayonet. Doctor Gindrey operated on him, gave him an artificial anus, and treated his ruined buttock. He survived his wounds and the following six operations. Today he is the faithful and tireless secretary general for the Association of Veterans of Dien Bien Phu.

The recapture of Éliane 1 brought us many casualties. Master Sergeant Boulier, hit in the legs and the left hand, spent the night in a hole that he tried to enlarge by digging with his good hand. At first light on April 11 he was brought to the unit on a stretcher. Fearing gangrene, Grauwin opted to amputate to save his life. Facing strong resistance from his patient, the doctor decided instead to operate. He reset the open fractures and fastened the legs together until he could cast them in plaster after all danger of infection had passed.

When it came to dressing the injuries of Gunther Jansen, I really needed the help of my assistant Sioni. The young German Legionnaire had an enormous wound in his lower back and an open fracture of his left femur. Because of the risk of infection, it was impossible to put him in a cast. His leg was immobilized in a short section of metal gutter that had to be held in the right position when I shifted him on his side to wash his back. The treatments were so painful that I gave him a shot of morphine fifteen minutes before I changed his dressings. Even then he screamed in pain. When Dien Bien Phu fell and I attended him for the last time, the wound on his back had almost completely healed. It had to be a miracle, when one thinks of the conditions—the heat and humidity and the mud that invaded the shelters and necessitated that we elevate the beds and the stretchers.

At the unit we could only keep the grievously injured who needed daily attention and nursing. Those whose condition had improved returned to their quarters and often back into combat. I tried to stay in touch with the wounded who were in nearby shelters by bringing them oranges, cigarettes, and condensed milk that Madame de Castries and the Red Cross sent us by parachute. These packages allowed me to stay in touch with many patients, even outside those shelters. I could find out if they were well or, if not, alert Doctor Grauwin to any problems. Thus I could follow the progress on the hand of Lieutenant de Wilde, who, wounded on March 30, had returned to a nearby unit. But the doctor worried on seeing me leave the trenches for these sorties, even though I always wore my helmet.

The assaults continued, although they were less violent than those of the first days of April. Every day brought us new casualties. When Lieutenant Colonel Langlais dropped by to bring cigarettes, Doctor Grauwin asked him to move the men of the GCMA (commandos) out of their quarters close by so that our unit could connect to the neighboring shelters once the engineers had dug an access under the road. Groupement de Commandos Mixtes Aéroportés was similar to the much later Vietnamese Civilian Irregular Defense Group (CIDG), controlled by U.S. Special Forces. The man I was later to marry, Captain Jean de Heaulme, was a member of GCMA working with hill tribes outside of DBP, although he was not at the camp itself during the siege. The commandos, autonomous intelligence agents in the Vietminh zone, had been pulled back to Dien Bien Phu from Lai Chau, but after the March 13 attack that entrapped us, they could no longer fill their role. New shelters were built in another section of the camp for them so that the quarters the commandos had occupied could greatly enlarge the underground hospital. To increase even further its capacity, the engineers carved out alcoves in the depths of the walls. Retrieved parachutes were placed on the benches that served as beds. It looked sinister, and we named those lightless tunnels the "catacombs."

Lieutenant Colonel Langlais, who commanded the central position, was truly the soul and mind of the defense of Dien Bien Phu. He was the actual leader. He was everywhere. His morale was extraordinary and his contempt for danger galvanized the men. "It is really Langlais who is the chief," Bigeard would later tell the journalist Jean Pouget, as quoted in Bigeard's book, *Pour Une Parcelle de Gloire* (For a Little Bit of Glory). Langlais was a man with all the qualities and the defects of a strong personality: irascible with a heart of gold. Having learned that, for three weeks, I had been sleeping on a stretcher that I set up between two patients, he ordered that a tiny shelter be dug out in the earthen wall of the new quarters, that it be tented with parachutes, and that it be furnished with a cot and a cane armchair. He presented it to me on his visit to the new unit. You can imagine my gratitude! I felt such extraordinary joy to suddenly have a corner to myself, and I was infinitely touched that this great soldier demonstrated such sensitivity.

In one of the shelters of the new unit, with four other casualties, lay Lieutenant Alain Lécué of the 6th BPC. He had arrived on April 18, his head drenched in blood. A shell fragment had penetrated his brain, and he could no longer speak. Grauwin believed nothing could be done and dropped this dreadful diagnosis: "He'll be dead in three hours." And then he decided to attempt the impossible. Deudon set Lécué up on the operating table and I took off his shoes while Sioni cut his hair. The doctor operated and removed a piece of bone from Lécué's skull the size of my open hand, as well as a cup of crushed brain tissue. Against all hope, Alain survived. After hours in the recovery room, he was placed, for lack of space, in that sinister, lightless tunnel. His suffering was intense, but after a few days, life took over again. Not being able to speak was very hard on him and I often went to see him. One day he showed me his letters from the mail dropped by parachute. He signaled that he wanted me to read them to him. He was still very young, but he was already married. Often he was overcome by emotions, and I needed to skip the most touching parts of his letters. I felt awkward in entering the intimacy of this young couple living such a rough period of separation and anxiety. Three days after the fall of Dien Bien Phu, when the Vietminh ordered the removal on stretchers of the injured to settle them under parachutes erected as small tents, I could not get close enough to Lécué to return his correspondence. As a result, when we had to prepare our bags to go into the prisoners' camp, I feared that this precious mail would fall into the hands of our guards and I tore up the letters and threw them into the Nam Youm River. How I regretted this act when, an hour later, the counterorder arrived: We were not leaving. Soon after Lécué was liberated with other officers, he was operated on again and recovered his ability to speak. When I saw him again in Paris, he asked me to return his letters, which I could not do. I was terribly distressed. A long time later Lécué told me, "You don't know what your presence meant to us. When you would pass by in the corridor we all tried to attract your attention, you were so cute in your para uniform!" (It had been given to me by a paratrooper so that I could wash my own uniform.)

Although I was not in charge of the many stabilized patients moved to the new units, the location of my little hideout among them allowed me to keep an eye on them and report any medical downturn. During the day it was the Vietnamese male nurses who came to administer the shots of antibiotics.

I didn't know every one of those wounded, of course, but some I knew better, such as Master Sergeant Larriaud, navigator of the Dakota that had brought me here the night of March 28. He was hit in the knee by shrapnel as he was carrying a casualty on a stretcher. I remember also Lieutenant de Cacqueray, his leg amputated in the surgical unit, who was brought to the new unit when his condition improved. His courage was magnificent.

Master Sergeant Boullier was none too happy because he had maggots under his cast and the odor bothered his fellow patients. No matter that Doctor Grauwin kept telling him that these little creatures were cleaning his wound; the itching was driving him crazy. In the same shelter lay Lieutenant Ruiter, taken back to surgery because of infected wounds and hemorrhage. When he returned to the new unit he suffered from dysentery and sensed that he reeked like a corpse. In his journal, he wrote, "With the rain, the trenches are filthy mud holes where it is impossible to circulate to get to the medics." And he added, "The only consolation, along with the good soups, are the cigarettes, the oranges, and the milk that nurse Geneviève de Galard brings us."

Many years later I was asked if, during certain moments of urgency, faced with the frightful task of triaging the wounded who could not all be operated on at once, or in cases that seemed irremediable, it had sometimes been decided to abbreviate the suffering of these men practically already dead. Never did I hear the slightest discussion of this matter during that time. All medical personnel had only one passion, one idea in his or her head: to save the man by all means possible.

Since I was assigned to the central medical unit, obviously I speak mainly of it in this chapter, but we must not forget that the same quality care was administered in the other units, such as that of Doctor (Captain) Resillot, parachuted into Isabelle on March 14; that of Doctor Vidal, set up on the banks of the Nam Youm at the foot of Éliane 4 on March 15; and that of Doctor (Captain) Hantz, parachuted at night under Vietminh artillery fire on April 7 and located to the south of the command post.

Chapter Six

TOWARD THE FALL

At the medical unit, day followed day yet always differed. After the major battles came moments of calm. Every war brings these contrasts between the tense pressure of conflict and moments of respite when life takes over again with the same habits, almost seamlessly; and in unusual situations, one savors the unwinding. At those times the injured could enjoy a visit from the doctor attached to their battalion or from their comrades.

The main surgical unit received all wounded, friendly or enemy. The enemy were treated just like the others, their wounds bandaged, plaster casts applied, and condition stabilized before being sent to the shelter for wounded Vietminh. Once they had recovered, they joined the group of prisoners utilized as the work force (PIMs). Because of the problems of language I could not converse with them. They were courageous combatants, and I never saw in the French medical corps any manifestation of animosity toward them. For us who had Vietnamese in our ranks who also were courageous and dedicated patriots, we had the feeling that they were living a civil war. Some of them had been trained under Ho Chi Minh thinking that he alone could lead them to their independence. Others had suffered from the rigid and terrorist methods of the Communists. As for me, I rather regarded these very young adversaries as victims when we learned of their commitment en masse in these assaults, which caused them horrifying losses in killed and wounded.

We often saw our wounded, who were closest to the central unit. The battalion doctors and medics administered first aid on the spot, sparing the lives of the wounded when artillery fire made it impossible to carry them to the unit. Some of them were dragged to the doctor by a buddy who tore them from death's grip, demonstrating admirable solidarity and brotherhood. In their infirmaries the battalion doctors administered first aid and placed broken limbs in casts, lessening the load on the unit surgeons. Doctor Grauwin often advised them over the telephone. Coordinating the treatments of the battalion medics, Doctor Le Damany, in liaison with the medical service in Hanoi, ordered parachute drops of bandages, medicine, and all the necessary matériel. Of the 1,460 wounded in Dien Bien Phu at the end of the fighting, 390 were in the units and more than a thousand were in the battalion infirmaries, which spared our main surgical unit from being completely overwhelmed by patients.

Occasionally, photographers and film crews came to visit the camp. Pierre Schoendoerffer, cameraman for Film Services of the Armies as well as author and director, told me years later, regarding his movie *Dien Bien Phu,* that in a scene where a feminine silhouette crosses the surgical unit, "I wanted to evoke your presence, because in that hell you were for me the image of Christian charity."

Daniel Camus, a photographer, asked me one day if he could follow me as I worked with the wounded, and if he could come with me to the enlargement of the medical unit we called the "catacombs," where he wished to photograph me with Second Lieutenant Lécué. Of course I accepted, happy to have a memento of my patients and of the unit. Unfortunately all his pictures were destroyed. Jean Peraud, another photographer, disappeared forever during an escape he attempted with Schoendoerffer, by jumping from a Molotova truck on the way to captivity after the fall of Dien Bien Phu.

On quiet days, once our work was done, we chatted or listened to the funny stories of the telephone operator, Julot Vandamme, as he regaled us with his sentimental adventures. Peals of laughter echoed in the corridor of the unit when he read us the letter from the tax collector in Roubaix demanding payment for a fine still owed when he left France! Julot never removed his helmet. He wanted to be ready to rush outside in case of failure of the phone or the generator. For years I did not know what had become of him until one day, thanks to Deudon, one of the unit medics, I discovered that he was living in Belgium. He was able to come to see me in Paris, and it was with great joy that we met again.

One of the happy memories of those difficult days is the April 23 arrival at our unit of naval lieutenant Bernard Klotz, promoted later to admiral. He was piloting a Navy Hellcat on a bombing mission over Éliane 1 when he was hit by Vietminh antiaircraft fire. Warned by his crew member that flames were coming out of the aircraft, he continued his dive, dropped his bombs, regained altitude to avoid crashing into the French lines, ejected four hundred meters to the south of Éliane 2, and touched ground twenty meters from an enemy trench. He hid in a trench, where a group of Legionnaires tried to reach him. At nightfall a Legionnaire succeeded in pulling him out and brought him to our unit to attend to his shoulder, injured when his parachute opened. On November 7, 2000, as President Jacques Chirac was awarding the Grand-Croix of the Legion of Honor to Vice Admiral Bernard Klotz, a funeral was being held for Sergeant Bleyer, who with two other sergeants had risked his life to save Klotz. There were at least two of us who thought of Bleyer that day with deep emotion.

On Klotz's arrival at our unit there was a joyous reunion. Doctor Gindrey and he recognized each other. They had been in grade school together. After attending to Gindrey's friend, in his honor Doctor Grauwin took out his last bottle of champagne. On leaving the unit, his arm in a sling, Klotz presented himself to Colonel Langlais, asking him "how a navy pilot, without plane or ship, may join the fight."

At Dien Bien Phu, the navy pilots and the air force fighters were heroes. Their diving attacks were very spectacular, and the pilots displayed undeniable courage. But perhaps it has been unfair to forget the prowess of the crews on the transport planes, who, constrained to land on defined axes, from the beginning of the battle were the prey of the Vietminh antiaircraft guns, the incredible density of which they were the first to discover. The parachute drops forced the planes to fly in on a certain vector at a reduced speed, and as the area held by the French shrank, they had to release their loads from higher and higher altitudes to lessen the danger, with losses and an increasing inaccuracy that the combatants on the ground did not understand. For the pilots it was always the same problem: to stay on the fixed axis, to slow down, and to see climbing toward them the trajectories of the shells that followed them relentlessly. They had to make several passes and returns until every paratrooper had jumped, without counting the risks they took during night flights. Or they had to land, all lights out, engines cut, to evacuate the injured under artillery fire.

One day I felt great joy when a young telephone operator offered me a chance to call Hanoi. It was dinnertime and I was able to reach Guite de Guyencourt, our chief flight nurse, at the mess. She happened to be there, but I could not hear her voice, and the Hanoi operator served as the connection; however, I shall never forget the extraordinary impression of feeling so close to my friends. At other times Guite climbed to the Citadel of Hanoi, where the telephone center was located, so that we could speak directly. Thanks to her my mother could receive news of me.

We lived other memorable events, such as the 1954 Easter Mass celebrated in the operating room of our unit, miraculously empty on that day. All who could walk came to join the injured lying in the recovery room, opposite the operating room. Father Yvan Heinrich was the celebrant. A great fervor filled the space; the closeness of death called us all to reflection and prayer. Many received Communion.

Day by day the area for the parachute drops diminished and posed problems for the renewal of our supplies of ammunitions, food, and medicines. Some of the packages fell into the hands of the Vietminh as the Dakotas turned to avoid the antiaircraft that had been deadly for days on end. Luckily for the injured, at the central unit we never ran short of medicine or bandages. Sometimes I heard Doctor Grauwin say, "We are running short of blood or plasma." Then a miracle would bring us some at the next drop.

Morale was holding up. We hoped that the rainy season would bring a halt to the fighting. Mud invaded the tunnels and the shelters and we had to raise the lower-level beds. Water seeped into certain places; the engineers dug sumps to collect the runoff, and one night, on my way from the wing to the central unit, I fell in mud up to my hips. Imagine the irony, when our use of water was limited and we had to use it sparingly even to keep clean. The muddy trenches made the carrying of stretchers increasingly difficult. The heat and the humidity caused painful irritations under the casts. Flies proliferated and maggots showed up in the bandaged wounds to cries of horror from the patients.

The number of troops was diminishing day by day. The number of reinforcements was insufficient and many of the injured soldiers returned to the fight, to our great admiration. Among the 4,277 men dropped as reinforcements beginning March 13, 680 volunteers jumped into Dien Bien Phu without having been certified as paratroopers. When one considers that they were not landing on a well-prepared drop zone but on blockhouses, trenches, and barbed wire, one can well call it heroism and a magnificent esprit de corps.

Despite the intense pace of caring for the wounded, we tried to keep up with developments in the conflict. Perez, one of the male nurses, was always gathering news and passing it on to us. We also received news from the doctors, from soldiers who came to visit their injured comrades, or directly, when I visited another unit during calm moments.

On the night of March 30 we followed closely the loss of the first three defense posts, Dominique 2, Éliane 1, then Dominique 1. Just as Lieutenant Brunbrouck was brilliantly blunting the Viet offensive, Lieutenant Luciani of the 1st BEP was desperately hanging onto the summit of Éliane 2 and galvanizing his men. Hope flowed anew. A counterattack was launched successfully on Éliane 1; Dominique 2 could have been retaken, but Captain Pichelin was killed and three of his men risked their own lives to recover his body. All that remained of these positions were bomb craters, and they could no longer be held. Attacks and counterattacks followed one another to successfully regain Éliane 2 with the support of several battalions and the tanks of Captain Hervouët, who, hit twice, arrived at our unit and returned to the battle with both arms in casts.

On the night of April 1, the drop of Major Bréchignac's paratroopers began. Their leader was an eminent figure among the paratroop commanders. The men were dropped in small units until the night of April 5. I can still hear Colonel Langlais' shouts of rage and disgust in the face of these reinforcements sent in driblets as by a medicine dropper and at the refusal of Hanoi to parachute the men anywhere but on a drop zone. The zone used earlier, the landing strip, was now completely under Vietminh fire.

Huguette 7 was attacked once again, lost, then retaken, thanks to the heroic combat of the young Vietnamese paratroopers under the command of Captain Botella. But the new reinforcements were so minimal that, his soul in agony, Colonel Langlais decided to abandon the post.

It was at that point that an odious event occurred. At noon on April 3 the Vietminh announced a half-hour cease-fire to allow for the removal of the wounded. The Legionnaires who advanced toward the enemy lines to rescue their comrades found no wounded, only four stretchers bearing their mutilated corpses. A fine example of psychological warfare. We were deeply pained by these orchestrated manifestations meant to show a power that fears no judgment or censure in an attempt to break its adversaries' morale. But by using the dead as victims, after giving the impression of a gesture of good will, the Vietminh provoked our repulsion at the horror of their inhumanity.

On the night of April 3 a large contingent of the Bréchignac battalion parachuted inside the camp. Lieutenant Colonel Langlais had won his case at last and, to mark the landing spot, ordered that a barrel of petrol be lit on a sandbank by the river, near the central sector. The night was clear and calm, allowing us to go outside and admire the spectacle of these white domes floating silently down from the sky. A young paratrooper landed close to our unit. As he stood and saw me, he exclaimed, "What do you know? There's a woman here!" His tone was almost optimistic, as though he was thinking, "So, it can't be as terrible as they told us in Hanoi."

While the counterattack on Huguette 6 was taking place, Sergeant Ney, hit on his tank "Nettlingen," was carried to the unit, his face covered in blood, his skull injured, and one eye torn out.

On April 4 Lieutenant Defline from the famous 8th BPC was pinned to the ground by a burst of gunfire that hit him in the shoulder and broke his thigh as he was rushing to the support of Huguette 6. To save him the paras of his battalion dug a trench into which they gently rolled him. Despite a morphine shot, he suffered agony as he was carried to our unit and endured the long wait in the central tunnel where the air was oppressive and unbreathable. Operated on by Doctor Gindrey, he woke up in a cast. "Above me," he said later, "the face of a woman was floating, and a good smell of warm soup. I didn't know it yet, but I had just been introduced to Geneviève de Galard."

I gave him injections of antibiotics daily and I watched closely for any signs of infection. Oddly, Jacques Defline kept drawing my attention to the small wounds on his neck due to shrapnel. I confess that, having a lot to do, I did not find them very important. Some time later I understood the reason for his worries when I learned that he was engaged to be married. Apparently he forgave me, since he asked me to be a witness at his wedding.

That night of April 4 the 8th BPC paid dearly. The stretcher bearers brought in Sergeant Lagarec, hit in the abdomen and the elbow. Already wounded in February and evacuated to Hanoi, he had volunteered to rejoin his company, as had his comrade, Sergeant Monchotte, who also was brought in with eight bullets in his kidneys.

As the x-ray machine no longer functioned, Doctor Grauwin could only administer antibiotics to Monchotte and keep him a few days in the unit before sending him back to his battalion's infirmary, where he remained on his cot until the end of the hostilities. Long after, he told me he owed his life to four paratroopers he didn't know from another unit. Seeing him fall, these men, inspired by a sense of brotherhood, started firing on his assailants and were killed in the process. It was to them that Colonel Le Mire dedicated his book, *The Sparrow Hawk*: "To the four silent companions of the night, forever unknown in their tomb of mud."

On April 5 the parachute drop of a new surgical unit was announced. It never arrived. The Vietminh had marked a false landing zone with fires and, in doubt, the pilot had decided not to drop the medics and flew them back to Hanoi.

On April 7 Doctor Hantz's unit was dropped at night under artillery fire. Hantz still remembers the tracer rounds spraying up to surround the aircraft and the reception of violent shelling upon touching the ground, some of his men falling on barbed wire, others in trenches. Hantz himself landed on the roof of a Dodge and crawled under it, waiting for a break that allowed him to recover his material, scattered about but still intact.

The announcement of the drop of paratroopers from the 2nd BEP during the night of April 9 evoked cries of joy that spread throughout the unit. And on April 10, Bigeard, who by all accounts, had an extraordinary sense of tactics, launched a counterattack on Éliane 1. From then on he directed the counterattacks, and Major Thomas took over the command of the 6th BPC. Bigeard, who would soon become a legend, could not fail. Hope was reborn. Among the injured, those who were able to walk watched from the unit entrance and followed the conflict from afar.

The attack started at 6:00 AM, and by 3:00 PM its mission was accomplished after a hard-fought one-on-one battle. Bigeard's reputation, well earned, grew again, along with that of the captains who participated in the fight and whose names now floated like a standard: Trapp and Lepage of the 6th BPC, Charles and Minaud from the 2/1 RCP (2nd Battalion, 1st Parachute Light Infantry Regiment), and Martin and Brandon of the 1st BEP, whose paratroop Legionnaires began to sing. When Bigeard decided to send in two companies from the 5th BPVN, the young Vietnamese paratroopers, who didn't yet have a national anthem, broke out in full voice with the Marseillaise. Tirelessly, the airmen of Captain

Charnod and the PIMs, bent under the weight of boxes, had been climbing the western slope of the combat base to resupply the combatants with ammunition.

These admirable exploits deeply impressed the wounded and the personnel of the unit. The courage of the soldiers raised the spirit of those who could no longer fight and found time dragging in the stifling shelters. I was often amazed by their morale.

I thought that they were supported by this omnipresent comradeship, as was I. As an example, the day that Doctor Grauwin cut open an abscess on my left shoulder caused by the humidity and the friction of a strap, Sioni, who helped me pass out the soup, decided to do this task alone so that I could relax and rest.

One day Colonel Langlais sent me a message that a large American press agency represented in Hanoi by Margaret Higgins was offering, by a terse telegram, to pay me thousands of dollars for an exclusive on my memoirs of Dien Bien Phu. It made me laugh, and I was so surprised that I knew not what to decide, other than to refuse any money for myself. Finally, preoccupied with my work, I simply never responded to that astonishing offer made during the worst of the battle.

The engagements that allowed the recovery of Éliane 1 were terrible. At the 6th BPC they counted fifteen killed, ten missing, and twenty-six wounded, including three captains. At the 2/1 RCP, Captain Charles and Captain Minaud were injured under a deluge of steel and fire. Charles' arm was shattered. A tourniquet was placed on his arm, and with another wounded man, supporting each other, they progressed through the trench, which the rain had transformed into a swamp. When they arrived at Doctor Vidal's unit, Charles collapsed from exhaustion. The following day he awakened to find himself with his arm enclosed in a chest cast. He later said, "The unit, overwhelmed with casualties, could no longer accommodate new arrivals and I had to leave. I was surprised to see a woman beside me. She removed her helmet and placed it on my head. Then she took my hand and led me to a shelter. It was Geneviève de Galard." The place I led him to was the "catacombs."

On April 13 Lieutenant Brunbrouck, who had saved Dominique 3 on March 30, was brought to the unit after Father Trinquant, the chaplain of Tactical Group No. 9, had given him absolution. Doctor Gindrey, his friend, could do no more than relieve his pain and stay by his side as life departed from him. His death hit the doctor very hard.

Toward mid-April the posts Huguette 6 and 7 were increasingly iso-lated by enemy trenches that the Viets had dug as close as possible to the barbed wire that surrounded the positions they planned to attack. Many coolies injured on their resupply runs were brought to us, and once again I saw my friend Loulou Martin.

On April 19, the day after Easter, Lieutenant Galopin from the 1/4 Regiment of Moroccan sharpshooters was brought to us. He had been wounded when his unit covered the PIMs as they tried to supply Huguette 1 under attack. It was he who undertook to bury the crew of Dartigues after his Dakota was shot down in late March. He recognized me first and recalled the burial of the airmen. He had been wounded in the back by an explosive and asked me if his injury was serious. I reassured him, as I hoped his strong constitution would save him. Sadly his wound was more serious than I thought, and during the night, despite all our efforts, he died without suffering. Father Heinrich administered the last rites.

At the Foreign Legion command post, Lieutenant de Veye informed me that his brother-in-law, who commanded Huguette 1, had been killed. His position, riddled with shell craters, its trenches obliterated, had been lost. Of this horrendous battle only one survivor remained, in such a stage of shock that he was unable to give any information.

By April 24 the Vietminh had 35,000 combatants, while there were only 3,250 able-bodied men left in Dien Bien Phu and 1,400 in Isabelle. They were exhausted and crowded in the mud of the trenches. How justly the garrison merited the citation on order of the French army that stated, "United by the will to win, officers, noncommissioned officers, corporals, and soldiers have earned the admiration of the free world, the pride and the gratitude of France." That same day Colonel de Castries was named general, Lalande and Langlais were promoted to colonel, and Bigeard and Seguin-Pazzis were promoted to lieutenant colonel.

On April 29 Colonel Langlais invited me to his command post. General de Castries wanted to give me something. When I opened the enve-lope he held out to me, I discovered two decorations: a Legion of Honor and a Croix de Guerre! My heart filled with emotion, but even more so when I learned that the decorations belonged to Colonel Langlais and Captain Bailly, who were letting me have theirs since the package con-taining those destined for me had fallen, along with several others, in enemy territory. At the same time I was handed the text of the citation, written by Colonel Langlais, whose words even now bring tears to my eyes: "Geneviève has earned the admiration of everyone for her quiet courage and smiling dedication. . . . With unmatched professional competence and an undefeatable morale, she has been a precious auxiliary to the surgeons and contributed to saving many human lives." And the last phrase left me speechless: "She will always be, for the combatants at Dien Bien Phu, the purest incarnation of the heroic virtues of the French nurse."

When Captain Bailly, although badly wounded in the leg, left after the fall of Dien Bien Phu for the prison camp, after my own liberation I sent Mrs. Bailly her husband's medal. I certainly owed it to him.

The following day, April 30, was Camerone, the traditional celebration of the Foreign Legion. The Vietminh wanted to celebrate this date in their own fashion, and their artillery opened noisily. But I was still able to join Colonel Langlais and Lieutenant Colonel Bigeard at the command post of Colonel Lemeunier. The latter honored me with the title of First Class of Honor of the Foreign Legion, along with Lieutenant Colonel Bigeard. Bursting with pride and joy by this expression of appreciation, I was now confident that the combatants considered me one of them.

Obviously not every man in Dien Bien Phu was a hero. It has been suggested that some broke down and some deserted. I witnessed none of that; therefore, I am unable to relate any such information. But one can only imagine what it was like to be in a unit dismantled by casualties in conflicts in which each soldier faced ten Viets, in which the unit's leader had been wounded or killed, and the individual was reassigned by luck of the draw to a new team. One cannot underestimate the shock effect of bombardments or of total exhaustion.

Extraordinary courage inspired a tenacious will in the men who could still fight. It benefited the garrison at Dien Bien Phu, so badly diminished in those last days of April, when the C-47s, despite the bad weather and the antiaircraft fire, still managed to drop paratroopers for reinforcement. Among them was Lieutenant Schmitt, future chief of all the armies, who, upon being apprised that Lieutenant Colonel Vaillant, the artillery commander, needed a communications officer, volunteered for the task.

It was a fine example of solidarity, among many others like it. At dawn on May 2, for instance, Major Guiraud of the 1st BEP saw three haggard men coming toward him, covered in mud and blood. They were carrying a fourth man, his legs torn apart, his face waxen. He was Lieutenant de Stabenrath. "In order to save him," Erwan Bergot wrote in his book *The 170 Days of Dien Bien Phu*, "Corporal Grana crawled along the trench, slipped under the barbed wire. Around him swarmed the *bodois*, the regular Vietminh soldiers. At the bottom of a hole half full of water and mud lay Alain de Stabenrath. Grana rolled in next to his lieutenant. Then, pulling him against his body, he grabbed him and carried him out backward."

From May 1 to 6 the battles raged practically without ceasing on the posts of Éliane, Dominique, and Huguette. The positions were being gradually choked by the Vietminh trenches. Conditions became dramatic for the injured. Many of them remained unconscious for hours in the mud of the foxholes without possibility of evacuation to the surgical units. Doctor Gindrey said that the mud even got into open abdomens.

Because of the rain, the parachute drop of Captain de Bazin de Bezons' 1st BPC, ordered by Hanoi and planned for the night of May 1, went very slowly, depriving the ground forces of the impact of a massive deployment, let alone having a bad effect on the troops' morale. The pilots of the eight C-119s decided to abort the drop due to the bad weather; they had trouble finding the drop zone. One part of the supplies fell among the Vietminh and the rest was hard to recover under artillery fire. On the defenders' hills, shelters crumbled under the rain and the shelling.

On May 1 we learned of the fall of Éliane 1, so brilliantly regained on April 10, as well as the fall of Dominique 3. At Éliane 2 the hand-to-hand combat continued as the men tread on the corpses. Captain Luciani, wounded three times, led the fight for Huguette 4, an enormous bandage over his eye. Patients left our unit, covered in bandages, to reinforce their comrades. The paratroopers continued to arrive. On the night of May 4 Captain de Bazin de Bezons and his command post rejoined his men, but a few hours later his leg was shattered by an enemy mortar. The new arrivals were amazed at how high the morale of the ground troops remained, as opposed to the low morale in Hanoi.

On May 3 General de Castries with Lieutenant Colonel Trancart came to visit the injured to congratulate them and award them well-earned citations. Unfortunately he could not decorate the men since the parachute that carried the medals landed outside our defense lines. The general was in shorts, wearing his Spahi red cap and a khaki shirt. On his shoulders were two stars on a red ribbon. Doctor Grauwin introduced the men to him and explained the circumstances of their injuries. The general expressed his regret at being unable to give them their medals, and Lieutenant Colonel Trancart handed them the text of their citation. After presenting his felicitations to the patients on our unit, General de Castries walked over to the underground wing of the hospital and splashed his way through the mud in the passage under the road. It was his first visit. Trancart tried to rush him so that he could be on time for a meeting of the battalion commanders, but the general wanted to visit every one of the wounded.

On the night of May 5–6 the transport planes succeeded in dropping a very large amount of supplies, but when the paratroopers resumed their drop, the antiaircraft fire became very active and the drop was halted at daybreak.

New attacks on Éliane 3 were repulsed by the 6th BPC and by the 1st BEP on Huguette 2 and 3, but the men could hear the noise of picks digging a tunnel under Éliane 2. A C-119, flown by an American, James "Earthquake McGoon" McGovern, was hit and exploded in enemy territory.

Suddenly, on the morning of May 6, a terrifying noise resounded, a sort of howl followed by an explosion. Someone said, "That is Stalin playing the organ." It was the sound made by rocket launchers called "Stalin's organs." A second time we heard the sound of these rockets.

An announcement was made: "The general attack will take place tonight, but it is impossible to recover the supplies of food and ammunitions dropped last night under the intense shelling." The assault against the two Élianes started as night fell, and at 11:00 PM an unbelievable explosion shook Éliane 2—the explosives that had been placed by the enemy under the post. It explained the tunneling heard by the soldiers earlier. The explosives piled in by the Vietminh caused an immense excavation. The battle went on all night. A counterattack succeeded, raising again a high wave of hope. One position was regained. Everyone sensed that the night would be decisive. The Élianes, overwhelmed, fell at dawn. The French artillery, lacking ammunition, had almost stopped firing, while Stalin's organs fired in relays and increased by tenfold the power of the Vietminh artillery.

It was the last night at Dien Bien Phu, the night I shall never forget. The battle was so intense that the injured could no longer reach our unit and had to wait where they fell until the usual lull at dawn. When my work was done around eleven at night, I stopped by the GAP 2 (2nd Airborne Group) to gather the latest news for my patients. As I started back toward my unit, Colonel Langlais said, "Geneviève, stay with us. You are our good luck charm; as long as you are here luck will smile on us."

After stopping at my unit, I returned to the GAP 2 command post. Lying on a parachute, I closed my eyes but couldn't sleep. I followed these tragic hours minute by minute, close to the radio. I shared with the combatants moments of high hopes, when a position was retaken by our men, and the awful moments, during the heartbreaking adieux of the unit commanders: "The Viets are thirty feet away. Give our love to our families. It is over for us." My heart tightened, as though I were hearing the last words of the condemned. Perhaps I should have had thoughts also of what was going to happen to me, a woman in the hands of the enemy, but I was thinking only of them. The emotion was too strong for me to consider myself.

By dawn all hope had disappeared. A breakout toward Laos was planned for that evening. General de Castries would stay behind to guarantee the safeguarding of the wounded. I returned to the surgical unit where the injured were to be brought in droves. That afternoon I learned that the breakout would not occur, as the last combatants were too exhausted. The fighting would cease to avoid the massacre of the wounded. The men were ordered to destroy by five o'clock everything possible, weapons and ammunition. Captain Hervouët was there, going from one man to another. At that moment François Willer of the 1st Cavalry Regiment raised high a bottle spotted with dirt: "My captain, there is no way that the Viets are going to celebrate their victory with our champagne." Hervouët agreed. Then, once the precious drink had been given to each sparingly, because of the large number of men, Hervouët added, "Let us drink to the freedom we are about to lose, to the satisfaction of having done the best we could to avoid getting where we are. You have no reason to blame yourselves. I will do my utmost to see that justice is done to you one day. Good luck!"

Later General André Mengelle, author of *Tanks and Men*, who was there at the time, would comment, "A moving toast and a strange vessel, where the men drink, with devotion, a symbolic draught in the cups they pass from hand to hand. They instinctively renew the ancestral ritual of communion of men welded together in shared ordeals. A last gesture of friendship, and for many, the ultimate goodbye."

Around four-thirty I walked over to say goodbye to GAP 2's officers. We all were close to tears. Langlais and Bigeard hugged me; others gave me letters and addresses. Back at the unit I informed my patients that the combat would stop at five. They were greatly relieved. I distributed the last cigarettes. Calm and a strange silence settled over the valley, and we waited.

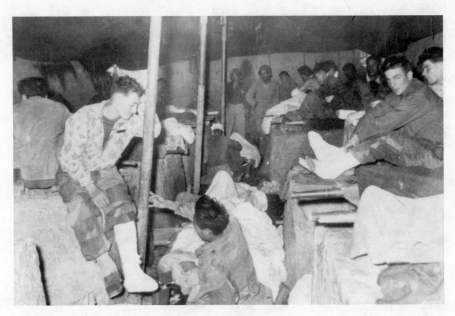

Triage room of the hospital. *ECPAD*

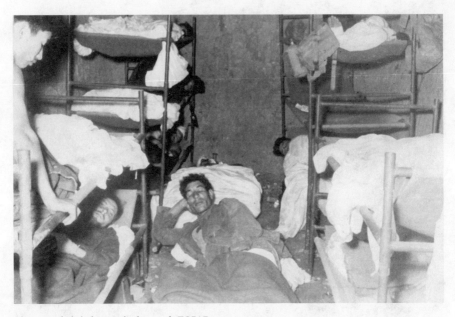

The wounded shelter in the hospital. *ECPAD*

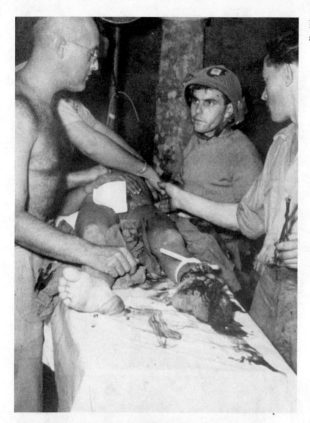

Doctor Grauwin performing an amputation. *ECPAD*

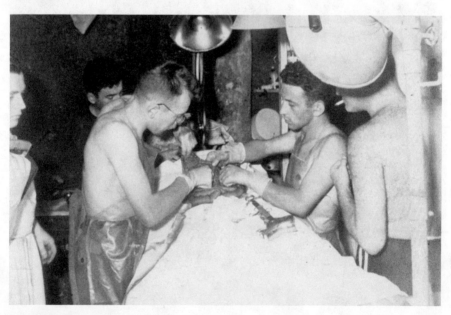

Doctor Gindrey (*left*) and Doctor Vidal (*right*) performing an abdominal operation. *ECPAD*

PARIS MATCH

N 271 DU 5 AU 12 JUIN 1954 50 fr

LA FRANCE
ACCUEILLE
L'HÉROÏNE
DE DIEN-
BIEN-PHU

My arrival at Luang Prabang on the day of my liberation. The legionnaires there rendered me honors. *ECPAD*

My great joy at being free. *ECPAD*

My departure from Luang Prabang. *ECPAD*

My welcome in Hanoi by General Cogny and General Dechaux. Here I shake the hand of Captain Jean de Heaulme, who two years later I would marry. *ECPAD*

A press conference at Hanoi. Well-known to Americans were the American journalist Marguerite Higgins (curly hair, back of head to camera) and the French journalist Lucien Bodard (seated behind Higgins in dark-rimmed glasses, smoking). *ECPAD*

My arrival at Paris-Orly on June 1, 1954, and my mother's joy. *Private collection of the author*

Receiving the Air Medal from Minister of Air Christiaens. *Private collection of the author*

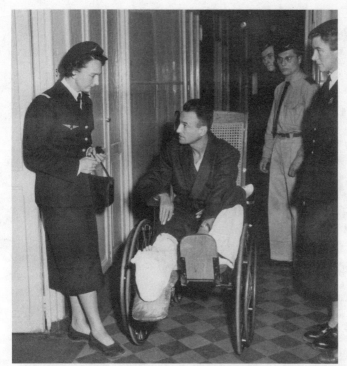

My visit to one of the heroes of Dien Bien Phu, Captain Cabiro, at Percy Military Hospital. *Private collection of the author*

My welcome to New York City on July 26, 1954, by Ambassador Richard C. Patterson Jr. Congresswoman Frances Bolton is in the auto. *Private collection of the author*

The parade up Broadway, riding with Congresswoman Bolton and Ambassador Patterson. *Private collection of the author*

I feel as if I were at the same time actress and spectator. *Private collection of the author*

My welcome at city hall, New York. *Private collection of the author*

I was accompanied by four very pleasant American military nurses during my entire official trip.
Private collection of the author

My arrival in Washington, D.C., by U.S. military aircraft provided by President Eisenhower. *Private collection of the author*

With Congresswoman Bolton, French ambassador Henri Bonnet, and Secretary of State John Foster Dulles in Washington, D.C. *Private collection of the author*

Greeted at the White House by President Eisenhower. *Private collection of the author*

Ready for the Medal of Freedom ceremony. Mamie Eisenhower is to my left. *Private collection of the author*

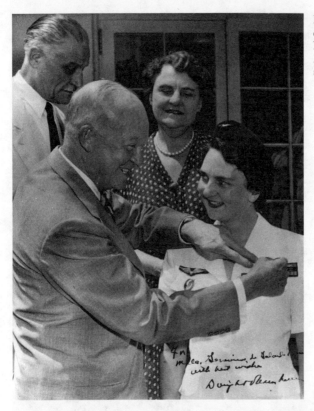

President Eisenhower
decorates me with the
Medal of Freedom.
*Private collection of
the author*

A magnificent
ceremony at Arlington
National Cemetery.
*Private collection
of the author*

My marriage to Jean de Heaulme at Church of the Invalides, Paris, June 14, 1956.
Private collection of the author

With François, our first born, at Madagascar, 1959. *Private collection of the author*

Our three children, François, Véronique, and Christophe, 1965. *Private collection of the author*

With two of my wonderful wounded veterans, 2000. [Simon Marie, the blinded soldier, stands with arm around author, near Rodez, France; Hantz Haas, the triple amputee, with the author at his home on the outskirts of Paris.] *Private collection of the author*

With General Marcel Bigeard in his study, 2004. *Private collection of the author*

My return to Vietnam in 2001. Jean and I are on the lake at Hoa Binh.
Private collection of the author

Chapter Seven

A HOSPITAL UNDER PARACHUTES

At about 5:30 in the afternoon of May 7, the Vietminh arrived running, without firing, and drove us out of the shelters, to the great despair of the wounded, who had to remain on their stretchers. I saw only from a distance the Vietminh who had given Major Grauwin the order to send everyone to the area designated for assembly.

At the unit Captain Lucien Le Boudec, wounded that morning, had just undergone an operation. He was still lying on the operating table when the Vietminh erupted into the room. One of them, wearing a helmet, sorted through the surgical instruments, and Le Boudec, hearing the noise, opened his eyes, causing terror in the man, who believed he was witnessing a resurrection. The captain was the last patient operated on by Doctor Gindrey.

As we emerged from the shelters, the embankment near the unit offered a vision of horror and I turned my eyes away. It was covered with bodies, turning purple and swollen, that no one had been able to bury in the past few days. After marching for 150 meters, we received an order to return to the unit. As we passed by a package of provisions that had burst open, Doctor Grauwin advised us to put a few cans of food into our pockets.

We crossed columns of prisoners who were already headed north. What a sickening and unnatural sight. And what humiliation for these men who had fought so courageously. Whoever met, in the acrid dust of that field lost in battle, those combatants, now prisoners, marching at a slow and heavy pace toward an unknown captivity, could never forget the weight that crushed their shoulders or the sorrow that filled their eyes. A German Legionnaire managed to reach me to say a few words, but he was quickly prodded on. Once freed, Gerhard Radzuweit regularly sent me New Year's greetings, and on the occasion of his receiving the Legion of Honor, he told me that the few words we shared as he was leaving that day were of great comfort to him.

Few French combatants had expressed hope that an end to the battle would come through negotiations at the Geneva Conference—the hope of an honorable exit that would at least avoid the suffering of countless wounded, who continued to suffer long and painfully and to pay with their flesh for an unjust captivity. Would not even the enemy have been relieved to avoid so many useless deaths? Alas, the two sides maintained their strategies: The French did not want the Vietminh taking over the Red River Delta; the Vietminh wanted to exploit to its limit the psychological dimension of the victory in order to conclude the accords in Geneva and to convince the Vietnamese, who remained hostile to them, of their unavoidable control over the entire country.

Some of my colleagues, including Doctor Gindrey, were worried for what might be my fate. I was not. At the time I could think of only one thing: We were rejoining our patients and would be able to care for them. When they saw us reappear, they expressed their joy. I could understand their fear of finding themselves alone with the enemy. During the night the Vietminh summoned Doctor Grauwin. When I saw him return at four in the morning he was extremely upset: "They are terrible, they made me sign . . . ," he murmured. I dared not ask him any questions, but I knew that only the interest of the wounded was guiding him. All the more determined to resist any pressure, I adopted an icy attitude when my turn came. I faced the Viet camp commandant and a delegate of the Communist Youth League. They told me that they summoned me because they knew that I took good care of the wounded, that they wanted my advice, that it was very important to maintain in my patients a sense of hope, that they were counting on me, and so on. The more they talked, the more I felt they wanted me to join them in a game that I could not quite figure out, and I kept repeating, "Since you speak of the humanity and the clemency of your president, the only humanitarian solution would be to authorize the evacuation of the wounded." They showed a certain annoyance at my obstinacy and sent me out.

In the early hours of the morning on May 8, the medics went out to retrieve the surviving injured in the outlying posts, pounded to ruins. They wrapped the dead in parachutes and carried them to the morgue. The injured who could walk left the shelter of the unit, happy to escape the suffocating atmosphere of the tunnels.

Father Heinrich went out to the Éliane posts with a doctor and a few male nurses in an attempt to recuperate the survivors of the last battle. Fathers Guery and Trinquand did the same at two other posts. At that moment Dien Bien Phu was a hallucinatory battlefield over which hovered the total silence of death. Everywhere they passed, the chaplains discovered the same horrible spectacle that had so struck me the evening before: putrefying corpses and amputees crawling toward the medical unit. As he searched for the injured, Father Heinrich witnessed the Vietminh filling in the trenches and, in this manner, burying the dead. Some of the Viet fighters noticed the chaplain's cross and offered him, as well as the medics, cigarettes. They were Catholics from Thanh Hoa, south of Hanoi. But the priest was denied permission to retrieve his possessions from his shelter, as was Father Guery, a former missionary who spoke Vietnamese and served as interpreter.

The bedridden wounded would have to endure three more days after the fall of Dien Bien Phu in their damp and muddy shelters, and I remained alone with Sioni to nurse them. Those three days left a horrifying memory. We no longer had electricity, and the Vietminh had emptied our stocks of bandages and medicines, particularly antibiotics, which were so essential. They took away our basins and urinals. I barely succeeded in hiding from them large bandages for those injured in the abdomen who had colostomies.

A leaden mantle had settled over us, even as the end of the fighting brought a certain relief. I had a difficult time raising the morale of the men, who as recently as the day before had been so courageous. The Vietminh made it a point of honor to organize a hospital under tents made out of parachutes, ordering the French to do the work. All the injured, some of whom had been brought back with the doctors who had already left with the prisoners, were regrouped at Dien Bien Phu. The doctors were placed in charge of triage of the very severely wounded, the moderately severely wounded, and the lightly wounded. Then the Vietminh separated the doctors from their patients, wanting to take over the care of the wounded to ensure their psychological control of them.

The installation of the injured, finally out of the shelters, took two days. During that time we were forbidden to approach them. Discreetly I tried to spot the tent where my abdomen patients lay so I could bring them the last bandages. Suddenly I found myself looking down the gun barrel of a young sentry. Not one more step, I thought, or I will surely be shot. Luckily a Vietminh doctor came up, asked me what I wanted and promised to have the bandages delivered to the wounded.

The attitude of the Vietminh became little by little less arrogant. In fact, we no longer had to deal with the politicians, and our contacts with their doctors were correct. We could communicate with them. Probably they felt much gratitude toward Professor Pierre Huard, the medical doctor who was the head of the French Red Cross and as dean of the faculty had trained most of them at the medical school in Hanoi. Because of their trust in him, he would soon be in charge of the negotiations for the liberation of the injured.

An area near the Nam Youm River was assigned to the personnel from the central unit, Doctor Grauwin and two medics. Doctor Gindrey was not on the list; he had gotten into an altercation with a guard that led to his joining the other prisoners. As for myself, our adversaries, shocked by the sight of a woman alone among men, wanted me to join the young Vietminh women who served food to the injured. I was very worried that I would find myself isolated among them. Grauwin and the medics protested, reminding their captors that I had been with them through the worst times and that they wanted me to stay with them. They even set up a small tent for me next to theirs. What would have become of me had I been separated from them?

I used that break to wash my hair in the river, to sleep, and to rest a little. The food consisted of rice and dry fish but it was sufficient.

After those two days of settling in, I was allowed to treat the wounded, but always in the presence of Vietminh combatants, under their guard, and under a parachute tent where, one by one, the wounded were brought on a stretcher. All I had for compresses were strips of torn fabric and some Mercurochrome, even though the French Dakotas continued to drop medicines, bandages, and food. One Vietminh doctor asked me to remove some stitches and watched me attentively as I worked. Perhaps he wanted to make sure that I was indeed a nurse.

On the other hand, I was not allowed to visit the injured in the other tents, especially not the officers, who had been separated from their men and regrouped along the riverside. I saw them from afar and could only make a few signs of friendship. Only Grauwin was allowed near them, called in by the Vietminh doctors to advise them on the case of Lieutenant Defline, who had just gone through a terrible time. When the prisoners assigned as stretcher bearers fetched him from his shelter at our unit, he was blinded by the light after five weeks in semidarkness. As he recovered his spirits he discovered a horrifying spectacle: In a chaos of gutted earth lay burned-out cars, opened cans of food, torn uniforms, and broken weapons half buried in the mud. His condition was getting worse, his injury bleeding under its cast. Despite injections of antibiotics administered secretly at night by Doctor Grauwin, the infection grew. The Vietminh doctors removed his cast and replaced it with a splint. Defline fell into a state of semiconsciousness. Called in at this stage, Grauwin stated that Defline could only be saved if he was evacuated. Defline became one of the rare officers to be freed, but he had to undergo amputation at the hospital in Hanoi.

Much of what I learned about our men taken prisoner came later from them, either in conversations with me or in their letters to me. In a letter to me, Captain Robert Charles, wounded in early April, evoked the atmosphere at the camp during the few days following its fall:

We pass one or two days without much happening. Then the Vietminh take us out of the shelters and regroup all the wounded. It is not a drama but a fresco from another era like the aftermath of the battle of Eylau under Napoleon; several thousands of wounded men in bandages, casts, bands of rags around their heads, leaning on wooden sticks, assemble in silence, a distant look in their eyes showing their uncertainty of the future. Small groups gather and every man inquires about the fate of his comrades.

These conversations are interrupted by a political commissar who goes from group to group haranguing them: "You are the confused soldiers of imperialism and of capitalism. You wanted to turn our people into slaves, you made them suffer. They have the right to treat you as badly as possible, but they are a generous people. We are going to take care of you. The least injured will put up makeshift tents from parachutes. For us, officers do not exist. We should punish them severely because it is they who have led you down this wrong path. We no longer want to hear a word about rank."

In the evenings the camp is invaded by thousands of coolies who methodically search everywhere: one team retrieves individual weapons; another the machineguns; a third the generators; then the radios, the batteries, the shoes, etc.

The wounded are left unattended. All medications have been requisitioned for their own wounded. Our doctors are helpless as they witness the suffering of the men they had saved. I was getting used to my chest cast when I had my first invasion of maggots. These little animals work conscientiously to clean out my wound, but their crawling around deprives me of sleep and I must make a few holes in my cast so they can get out.

The endless days dragged in the camp, without any news. The last to arrive in the Far East or at Dien Bien Phu shared with their comrades the little news they could recall.

Second Lieutenant Latanne, injured on the night of May 6, was among the prisoners from Éliane 4 brought back to the tent hospital. Under the prodding by the *bodois*, the enlisted Vietminh soldiers, and at the cost of horrendous pain, he hopped on one leg along a muddy trench, then sat down and dragged himself backward. In no time his bandages were soaked in mud. Ignoring their, "Maolen, maolen!" ("Quick, quick!" in Vietnamese), he stopped, exhausted, as the Vietminh soldiers, indifferent, kept going. Latanne was alone on the ground, dying of thirst, and remained there three days. Finally he dragged himself to the river, lost his balance, and passed out. He was saved from drowning by Doctor Rouault, attached to his unit, who left the column of prisoners to attend to him at the risk of being shot by the guard. After changing Latanne's bandages, the doctor, Major Botella, and two others fabricated a stretcher to carry him to a Vietminh infirmary, but they were soon exhausted, and the halting motion became too painful for the patient. This occurred on the evening of May 7; it was not until May 9, at night, that coolies carried him back in a net to Dien Bien Phu. He was suffering atrociously, unable to rid himself of the flies that covered his bandages, unattended for two days and totally dehydrated. He lived in absolute agony through May 10, when a last portage brought him to the temporary hospital where he rejoined his comrades. At last he could eat, drink, and be nursed.

The day before Staff Sergeant Legrain had also been brought under the parachutes and classified among the critical cases. On May 7 the Vietminh forced him to come out of the shelter, despite the cast that held his fractured leg. He could only drag himself, leaning on a stick, in terrible pain from his leg and from an intense thirst. On May 8 he rejoined a small group of wounded, among whom was a man lying on a stretcher, unattended, as a swarm of flies attacked his shredded legs. Legrain wanted to help but could do nothing and had to march on toward the so-called hospital designated by the Viets. Exhausted, he stopped. A Viet soldier passed him, turned back, and gave him a ball of rice and a piece of meat; he offered him his canteen of tea and told him of the clemency and humanity of President Ho Chi Minh. At noon on May 9, Legrain could not go another step, lay down in a pretty clearing, and fell asleep. About three in the afternoon he awakened to the sound of voices—the French returning to Dien Bien Phu to repair the landing strip so the injured could be evacuated. They bore stretchers made of bamboo and carried him back to camp. He hoped to rejoin his comrades, but instead, as he found himself alone after their evacuation, he was directed toward a corral of barbed wire where the officers were imprisoned and guarded by sentinels.

On May 10 Lieutenant Ruiter and the other casualties from the underground shelters of the GCMA emerged into the light of day and came to the hospital. On May 13 Lieutenant de Stabenrath died. I can still see him four days earlier, lying under a makeshift tent, pale as wax and in such a state that I doubted he could survive much longer. Yet he still had to endure three more horrible days, during which he was carried by stretcher to catch up with the column of prisoners, and then carried back to Dien Bien Phu. Badly dehydrated by dysentery, the care he received from the Viets came too late to save him. The Vietminh, wanting to demonstrate their humanity, were making it a point of honor to manage as best they could a difficult situation caused by the very large number of casualties. But where had the medicines dropped in by parachute gone?

Captain Le Boudec found himself in the same tent as Jacques Defline, who was lying in the adjoining cot in very bad shape. Along with Lieutenant Ruiter, Le Boudec kept watch over Defline during the long hours of his semiconsciousness. The Viets who nursed them wore prophylactic masks. Their care, Le Boudec later said, was basic but meticulous. Several among the wounded noticed the difference—as I myself did—between the attitude of the politicos and that, far more humane, of the health personnel and their aides. Many of the injured appreciated being washed for the first time in several days, even if the time for these ablutions, sometimes in the middle of the night, was not necessarily well chosen. Le Boudec found the Vietminh caregivers attentive to their patients, at least as long as he was in Dien Bien Phu. Young women, in uniform and masked, helped the injured to move about and brought them meals that seemed appetizing after weeks of military rations.

Under the tents morale was holding up. Bailly, severely wounded in the leg on the last night of battle, brought cheer to the men. He sang, and memories of his refrain still bring laughter: "Ah, how sweet it is to be caressed like cats, when we are captured by democrats!" General René de Bire, a lieutenant at DBP and today president of the National Association of the Combatants of Dien Bien Phu, taught his comrades the words to the songs of Georges Brassens: "When Margot unhooked her blouse . . . ," "Watch out for the gorilla . . . ," and so on.

The Vietminh focused its effort on propaganda. Several times we were brought together to watch movies on the Berlin Congress, the Viet war effort, and the construction of a Russian canal. A medical student and a women's delegate tried to indoctrinate me, all while demonstrating kindness that embarrassed me, especially when they wrapped their arms around my shoulders.

During the general assemblies, our enemies told us of the clemency of their president, of the humanity of their government. They criticized the imperialist occidentals and blamed the French for the delays in the talks for the liberation of the wounded, saying, "You see, now that you are beaten, your government is abandoning you." These large gatherings gave us a chance to approach a certain number of wounded men who had been separated from us and allow us to raise their morale as they saw the days go by without any progress.

From the camp we observed the reenactment and filming of certain battles by a Russian cameraman. The actors were all Africans or North Africans who were paid for their services in cigarettes and food.

On May 13 hope rose in the hearts of the wounded as they heard a helicopter approach. On board were Professor Huard, Doctor (Colonel) Chippaux, and Doctor (Colonel) Allehaut, who came to negotiate the evacuation of the injured. The French doctors who had been taken prisoner then returned to Dien Bien Phu to triage the wounded and spotted the helicopter from afar on their way to the prison camp along with the chaplains.

On the afternoon of May 14, eleven injured men were evacuated by helicopter. However, on the same day a de Havilland Beaver was damaged on landing. Doctor (Lieutenant) Arrighi, chief of the medical unit based in Luang Prabang, was on board. The Viets refused to allow him to go near the wounded. On May 15 and 16 not one helicopter showed up, not one Beaver landed, and the morale of the injured was affected as the Viet soldiers never stopped accusing the French of ignoring their fate.

The wounded men were often invited to sign petitions to invoke the clemency of President Ho Chi Minh and to beg for their freedom. I too was solicited to write the leader. On May 16 a member of the Vietminh called me to his office and announced that Ho Chi Minh had decided to free 703 prisoners in celebration of his birthday. He hinted at the possibility of further liberations and pressed me to write his president for his birthday. I answered that I wanted to think about it.

That set up a real conflict of conscience and I could not fall asleep. After asking the advice of several doctors and a few patients, I decided to do it, afraid that a refusal might compromise their freedom. That alone was worth more than my pride. My letter avoided the problem as I wrote Ho Chi Minh, thanking him for the freedom he decided to grant. I expressed my hopes for peace, hopes that I shared with the majority of men who have experienced the horrors of war. As I saw it, the letter had no political import; it was a letter from a nurse whose only concern was to help her patients, for whom evacuation was becoming more critical with each day. But of course my letter was edited before its publication and announced only as a good-wish message to Ho Chi Minh on his birthday. I found it very hard to take, but looking back I would do it again because the liberation of my patients, and hence their survival, was at stake. In any case, after their liberation I received letters of approval from the bravest officers in the camp.

On May 18 eighteen wounded were evacuated, but among them was not one officer or Vietnamese, and our hope was mixed with anxiety because the French government had demanded that a certain number of injured Vietnamese be liberated. On May 19 the celebration of Ho Chi Minh's birthday brought on long speeches and a holiday spirit among our guards. But during the military parade we saw with great sadness the remaining French tanks, "Mulhouse" and "Smolensk," decorated with portraits of Ho Chi Minh. On that same day eighty-four wounded men were evacuated. Haas, my dear triple amputee from the 2nd BEP, was among the first to leave, followed by Serge Genty and Simon Marie, the blinded young man we had nursed in our unit.

On May 21 the Vietminh announced my own liberation with manifestations of joy. However, I refused to leave my patients behind when I could still nurse them and support their morale. Besides, I did not want to take the place of one of them in a plane. So I requested that they postpone my trip until the end of the evacuations, and they allowed it.

On May 22 Professor Huard, who was aware of the difficulties in negotiating in the present context of international propaganda, took the precaution to write my mother a subtle letter of double meaning that he sent from Hanoi by certified mail. He warned her and asked that she use her best discretion regarding the evacuations. He led her to understand the official position she should hold:

> I am forwarding you a letter from your daughter that was entrusted to me yesterday in Dien Bien Phu. You may count on her being liberated in the near future, although not by my own doing. It is due to the clemency of Ho Chi Minh because of a letter she sent him on his birthday, May 19. I mention this so that an untimely article in the press does not confuse everything. Whatever your opinion or mine may be, it is essential that we play the game by the rules imposed on us. We do not want the liberation of the hundreds of prisoners still being held to be compromised.

Seventeen evacuations proceeded irregularly over the next few days. On May 26 Professor Huard finally obtained the liberation of 65 Vietnamese among the 150 wounded. They were the last of the 858 wounded to be freed.

On May 24, two days before the last evacuations, the Vietminh forced me to leave despite our agreement because international opinion was suggesting that they were holding me against my will. I had to obey, but I felt very sad that, after eighteen days of shared captivity, I had to leave behind not only my patients but also Doctor Grauwin and the medical staff. But they were happy for me and expressed their friendship. Before I left I bid them au revoir; I hoped to welcome them very soon in Hanoi.

The doctor and Julot, the unit telephone operator who had known so well how to make us relax and laugh during the darkest moments, accompanied me to the small Beaver, where Professor Huard awaited me. Two young Viet girls were also there, showering me with good wishes for me, my family, and my country. With tears in my eyes I hugged Doctor Grauwin and Julot. As I walked away Julot called out, "What is going to become of us now, without our blue eyes?"

Chapter Eight

FURTHER THAN HELL

When I learned that the liberations had ended I was already in Hanoi, where I rejoined the released wounded. But I often worried about the two hundred men still prisoners in Dien Bien Phu, and about their despair when they realized that they were not going toward the airfield but toward the Vietminh camps.

Even though I was no longer among them, I could not keep silent about their suffering or the life they endured. Several books and articles have since revealed the conditions under which they were led on the "long march," and then their captivity in the prison camps, as well as the astonishing number of mortalities there. But the fate of the injured prisoners not surrendered by the Vietminh during the exchanges was not known outside their family circles. Among them were many patients I had nursed. I received so many of their testimonies that I feel the obligation to share publicly their ordeal, too often untold.

There were several reasons for this silence. At first our government did not want to risk compromising the Geneva Accords, signed in 1954. Also there were the pitiful justifications for stopping a "dirty war." Private associations took over the task of responding to the helpless families. Madame Bidault, wife of the minister of the Foreign Department, took it on herself to open an office where the families of the prisoners could be welcomed and receive news. After my liberation I met Madame Lalande there; her husband, Colonel Lalande, had commanded the post Isabelle at Dien Bien Phu.

What the survivors wanted me to know, I now repeat with their approval and that of their families. There is no question that a large number of the wounded, captured before the battle had ended, were not brought to a medical unit and had to march toward the camps. Many died on the road.

On May 26 the injured, who remained under the parachute shelters in Dien Bien Phu and had not been released, left for the prison camps, some on stretchers, others piled one on top of the other in Molotova trucks made in Russia. Those on stretchers were loaded first in layers; fifteen or sixteen other wounded were loaded on top of them, howling in pain as the truck bumped along, especially when their broken bones grated against each other. The men were packed so tightly that, at first, they believed they were being taken on a short trip to the landing strip for evacuation. Imagine their distress and revulsion when Le Boudec, Latanne, Ruiter, and others realized that the Molotovas were heading north on the road to Tuan Giao. Yet they had been assured of their freedom.

In fact they were stopped as soon as they reached the edge of the valley. The Vietminh wanted to proceed with a general disinfection; ten liters of disinfectant for each vehicle were carelessly tossed over the men. Night was falling and so was the rain. The mood was sinister.

Three hours later the convoy reached the first camp. Its shelters were low, open to all the winds, and barely covered with branches and elephant grass to fend off the rain. The injured splashed through the mud toward the stalls. Staff Sergeant Legrain, who had arrived the day before, had fallen asleep in the rain, rolled up in a blanket. When he stood to survey the area, his crutches sank into the spongy ground. There hovered over the camp an odor of humidity, of mold, of rotten flesh, the smell of death. No one attended to the wounded except to submit them to a thorough search. The Vietminh soldiers confiscated all personal articles, money, knives, paper, and so forth.

Morale was at its lowest ebb when suddenly, in the silence, "two Legionnaires start singing. They are Slavs, their two voices blend together and I receive a lesson in optimism. We need it!" recounts Lucien Le Boudec. "The stalls are built of twisted logs, irregular and unshaped. The shelter is a mockery and the rain never stops. Besides, there is not enough room. I am squeezed between Charles, wounded in the right elbow whose cast cannot dry in this humidity, and de Wilde whose right hand was half torn off. Our wounds are unattended, our soiled bandages smell bad and we have to agree to turn over together as one man whenever we want to relieve our stiffened limbs."

Captain Charles has a memory of a place, he says, where "we are waiting either for death, or an improvement in our health before undertaking another march toward another camp." Care for the injured is nonexistent: "The number of prisoners shrinks on its own either in hospital or on the trail. I shall never forget the physical and morale distress of the severely wounded men. I visit them twice a day to lift their spirits. In these situations, one must not give in to despair, but must believe in life." Doctor Gindrey, Le Boudec, and his comrades stood by helpless at the deathbed of young Lieutenant Delafontaine, severely wounded in the hip and left without any care.

The fate of the injured Vietnamese, who had fought with such courage, is even less enviable. "They are treated by their Viet 'brothers' like pestilent animals," Charles testifies. "They implore me with their eyes to do something for them. Whenever I can, surreptitiously, I bring them some food. The fate that awaits them is unimaginably cruel."

Second Lieutenant Latanne also remembers that first camp, located between Dien Bien Phu and Tuan Giao, as a place where the wounded reached the nadir of distress. The rain, the mud, the minimal food rations, and the lack of medical care all added to the immense deception of not having been freed despite the promises of the Vietminh. Latanne retains the horrible vision of a young paratrooper lieutenant, his head leaning to one side, shot when he tried to escape and exhibited as an example.

The injured soldiers from post Isabelle rejoined those from the central position in this field "hospital" situated north of Dien Bien Phu. They told their comrades of the fire that consumed the first-aid post on May 7 and the panic that ensued. Men wounded in the abdomen and operated on a few hours earlier were seen tearing off their IVs and fleeing, holding onto their bellies while trying to carry their mates stuck in their stretchers. A few hours later the empty post finished burning.

At this time in the camp shelters, infection ran rampant because the bandages were not changed, and the smell was becoming intolerable. One day the Vietminh soldiers decided to proceed with a general bath in the Nam Youm, which ran near the camp. "We go there," Pierre Latanne relates, "in a pitiful procession of wretched men in rags, torn clothing, crawling, limping, some hobbling on one limb, others with slow steps, mutually helping each other. I go backward, seated on the ground, pulling myself by the arms so that my inert legs can follow." It was Lieutenant Planet who, despite his serious chest wounds, helped Latanne and scrubbed his back with sand, for lack of soap.

Meals consisted of a ball of rice and some guava tea—a far cry from meals in Dien Bien Phu under the parachutes, where well-seasoned buffalo meat was highly appreciated. Here every prisoner had a right only to seven or eight hundred grams of rice a day.

In the camp the injured with stronger limbs, who could move about, helped those unable to walk and did the chores without complaint, fetching rice or water. The first cases of dysentery occurred at this time.

The wounded had to elect a group leader since the French military hierarchy had been abolished. "Unanimously," explains Le Boudec, "we designate Lieutenant Datin, who can walk and who will serve as liaison with the Vietminh."

At the end of May our enemy began to send off toward Tuan Giao, about a hundred miles away, all the injured who were able to walk. Sergeant Monchotte, hit in the kidneys by bullets that had not yet been removed, walked bent over, and the Viets decided to take away the two sticks on which he leaned. Doctor Gindrey succeeded in convincing them to let him keep them. During the entire march Monchotte received no care and washed his wounds himself in a river along the way.

Charles and Datin set off on foot, and yet the latter had a bullet in his chest and shrapnel in his legs. Staff Sergeant Legrain, who still suffered from his broken limb, was considered cured and also sent off on foot, without shoes, supporting his weight on a bamboo stick.

When only the stretcher cases were left, the Molotova trucks reappeared and the loading of the injured in layers resumed. The trucks set off at night in horrendous conditions due to the ruts in the road. Two injured soldiers died during the journey.

At the first stop the men wounded in the legs lowered themselves from the trucks and proceeded on crutches to reach the spot that was assigned to them. There were only three sets of crutches, and Le Boudec was chosen to carry them back and forth so that all the wounded could be assembled. Luckily his calf injury was not too painful, but as he hobbled along he passed too close to a fire being lit by a Viet, who then threatened him with a stick. Le Boudec's reaction was swift: "I hold my crutches in my left hand and engage my adversary in a game of fencing. This does not amuse the convoy leader, who intervenes and condemns me to twenty strokes with a stick, applied as I am seated, bare-chested, my arm and chest in bandages. There is no longer a question of resisting, but murmurs rise from the group of my comrades. I have to ask them to keep quiet and I undergo the prescribed punishment."

The semi-invalids reached Tuan Giao about June 15 after a very arduous march on a difficult mountain road ravaged by bombs. Those wounded in the legs struggled in the descents and those injured in the lungs were breathless on the ascents. On top of that they endured heavy showers. In one spot the road was gutted by the rains and by the passage of numerous convoys. The Vietminh had repaired it with wooden logs covered in mud. Barefoot, Legrain slipped and clenched his jaws in pain and rage as he thought of the Vietminh injured prisoners conveyed in helicopters to the French hospital in Lanessan. Sometimes the men detoured through forest to avoid certain portions of the trail cratered by our bombs. Leaving the road to Lai Chau, they penetrated the brush in a dark wood on the flank of a hill and arrived at camp Tuan Giao.

At their arrival they were met by the *can-bo*, the political commissar. Mr. Ky Tu addressed them in these words: "Do not forget that you are prisoners of war, murderers, mercenaries, valets of the French colonialists and the American imperialists." Ky Tu, a rather important member of the Vietminh hierarchy, was tasked with the indoctrination of prisoners. He was attached to the sadly notorious Camp No.1, which was so masterfully described by the journalist-author Jean Pouget in his 1969 novel *The Manifesto of Camp No. 1.*

The prisoners had been told to expect a "field hospital." Charles felt the term was incorrect and that it was better called a death camp. "In a large square area," he recalled, "carpeted with thick vegetation that allows no sun to penetrate, where rain water drips ceaselessly, in the miasma of infected wounds and excrement from dysentery, our Viet 'protectors' had built a platform of logs raised two feet off the ground to isolate us from the soil." On a slight incline, the camp consisted of four barracks surrounding a rectangular area where the sun did not reach under the tall trees. The noncommissioned officers and the metropolitan soldiers occupied the lower barrack, the North Africans, the Vietnamese, and the T'ais the upper one. The officers occupied one barrack on the side, and the Legionnaires were lodged opposite. They were, in fact, huts rather than barracks.

Right away the officers were isolated from the other combatants. Nevertheless Le Boudec and Latanne were secretly visited by a Vietnamese soldier from their company who brought them tobacco. In the center of the court a sort of rotunda served as a consulting room for the doctor who came every morning wearing a gauze mask, and received his patients in a well-established order: first the North Africans, then the Legionnaires, then the French—the enlisted before the officers—and only then, voluntarily placed at the end like pariahs, the T'ais and the Vietnamese. The doctor hardly raised his eyes to the patients, and never touched them, but wrote in a notebook and distributed parsimoniously a few medications. Then he would leave, very dignified and almost mute, followed by male nurses, to make the rounds of the "immobilized." In the large barrack designated "Infirmary," the bandages were changed every ten or fifteen days and cleansed with Dakin. When a cast was too soft from the leakage of an open wound, it was eventually replaced. The "bandages" were pieces of parachute or shreds of rags washed twice and boiled under the oversight of the French doctors.

Latanne suffered excruciatingly from the wound in his leg. He was allowed an occasional morphine shot, which alone could alleviate his pain. Immobile on his cot, he was the prey of flies, as were the others who could not move. Flying in a pattern from the latrines to the wounded and the kitchen, they carried under their feet a myriad of germs. They massed on the dirty and smelly bandages, which emitted an odor of putrefaction. On one of his visits the Viet doctor ordered Latanne's bandage changed; his leg was swollen and purple and the dressing foul. The change was just in time: The flesh was black, puffy, and putrid. His wound was cleaned only with the detergent Dakin, which did nothing to relieve the pain but made him feel that he no longer reeked of death. As the leg was getting worse, the doctor decided to operate. Latanne was granted, "thanks to the infinite clemency of Uncle Ho," a spray of Kelene, which produced a freezing effect for a few seconds. "The effect had worn off and he kept on butchering me," Latanne recalled. "Held down by five Viets to keep me still, I believe that I screamed. It was too much pain all at once. I was on the verge of passing out. He dug around for a long time. 'This is what was causing you so much pain, a fine piece of metal,' said the surgeon, holding it up triumphantly. I asked if he could save it for me, which he did."

Latanne was not the only one to pass through the hands of the surgeon. Planet, whose torso had been perforated by shell fragments, had
pus throughout his lungs. The doctor pushed a drain guided by a metallic stem deep and brutally into the largest wound in his back. Planet
clenched his teeth and staggered, saying, "Whore! How that hurts!" Le
Boudec's wound was blooming into small fingers of pink flesh that were
cut off with scissors. It was amazing. All this occurred in the absence of
the only French doctor left at Tuan Giao, Doctor Premilieu, after Doctor
Gindrey had been sent to another camp with Captain Charles.

In the camp at Tuan Giao dysentery was wreaking its havoc, Latanne
relates. The injured who were able to walk with crutches and canes had
to get up several times at night, hobbling and limping, to deal with their
pressing needs. Their progress turned into an ordeal when it rained,
which was very often during this period of monsoon. The path that
led to the latrines was a cesspool of mud and excrement, as many were
unable to reach their destination in time. Without light at night, too often
under the rain, and with the threat from the sound of the guards' guns,
these nightly expeditions became a nightmare. Some of the men resolved
the problem with woven baskets filled with ashes from the cooking fires
that they kept near their cots. They emptied them at dawn and washed
them in the river.

Those who couldn't get up used old ration tins that the more ambulant emptied for them. "When the latrines are full," Latanne explains,
"the Viets assemble the stronger invalids, able to maneuver a shovel and
a pick, to cover the old latrines with earth and dig fresh holes." The
latrines consisted of a large ditch dug into the ground and crossed by two
boards twenty-five inches apart, precariously slippery from their usage.
The surrounding air was unbreathable.

A major prophylactic campaign was undertaken against the fly population. "They give each of us a bunch of bamboo slats that we must
weave into fly swatters," continues Latanne. "'The only ones of you who
will be allowed to eat are those who bring twenty-five dead flies!' declares
the camp commandant." Those who had killed dozens of flies, attracted
by their nauseating bandages, offered them to their mates so they could
reach their quota.

At Tuan Giao "the indoctrination lectures are boring, annoying,
but have the advantage of helping time pass," Le Boudec remembers,
"especially since each meeting was followed by a 'free' discussion, free

but obligatory on the subject just covered." One day Legrain, during a conversation more open than usual, received a powerful slap for having burst out laughing and had to perform self-criticism. (This was a system the Communists also used on their own men, all the way down to the basic three-man cell. Periodically a person was required to publicly analyze his or her shortcomings as a good soldier of the Cause and give an explanation of how he or she would improve. After receiving the group's comments, the repentant sinner would then join in the group's criticism of others. Every Vietminh unit down to battalion level had, in addition to a commander, a political officer who often led or oversaw the sessions.) Nonetheless, the days were desperately long, without any news or radio. Everyone had to make an effort to talk of things other than food or cars; someone who had a specialty or a hobby took the stage to discuss dove hunting, rugby, parachuting, or mountain climbing.

Singland, one of the wounded, who loved to sing and did it well, decided to fight boredom by any means. He created a sundial by planting a stick vertically in the ground. Another, Captain Bailly, who had given me his Legion of Honor medal so that I could be decorated in Dien Bien Phu, contributed his sense of humor, his smile, his kindness, his optimism, and his insurmountable morale. In a cast that reached from his groin to his toes, he entertained his neighbors by wiggling the cast like a puppet, with the help of a parachute line, as the plaster had been so softened by the fluids draining from his open fracture. Bailly talked to his puppet creation and the scene was hilarious, his comrade, Legoube, said. When Bailly started narrating the unbelievable adventures that he had already experienced, this young captain, a former British secret agent during World War II and counterespionage spy for France, officer of the Legion of Honor at twenty-nine, communicated to his mates some of his strength of character.

In the officers' barrack, but for a few exceptions, a great spirit of mutual aid reigned, particularly among the men from the same corps. The cohesion among the paratroopers, and among the Legionnaires, was exceptional, perhaps somewhat less in regard to the others. Latanne remembers how helpful his comrade Raymond Delobel was when the condition of his leg was worsening, "forcing him to eat, to come out of his deadly isolation." With a fierce will to hold on, to not let go, each man forced himself to stay clean, to shave at least twice a week, to wash out his dish after each meal, even if the chore fell always to the same people because the officer group had suffered the greatest percentage of those injured in the lower limbs. Because Le Boudec's right hand was in a cast, with his left hand he used on his mates a barely functioning pair of hair clippers that pulled their hair and did not evoke many thanks. The metallic gutter we had made for Captain Trapp, no longer of use to him, was transformed into large spoons, quite useful for eating neatly. The officers tried to use their intellect. Unfortunately there were only three books in circulation in the camp: a novel by Paul Vialar, *The Great Pack*; a handbook in Italian; and an anthology of French poetry from the Middle Ages, sadly quickly confiscated by the Vietminh. Some prisoners played cards cut out from the pages of a small notebook. Others, to play checkers, used stones as tiles on a board drawn in the dirt.

"Never is the officers' barracks quiet," Legoube attests. "The heavy, muggy air that stagnates under the trees never manages to cast its gloom over this group. The men stir the conversation, they sustain it so that it never goes out. It is like a fire, a flame that pushes back the darkness of solitude and prevents its octopus from wrapping its tentacles around us." Knowing the conditions for those injured men lying on cots made of wood rounds under leaky roofs of branches, poorly fed, my heart is full of admiration and empathy as I read these accounts that were entrusted to me by those who survived.

Sometimes the prisoners of that place became poets. Those who had the chore of fetching water from the river because they were in better shape said they appreciated the beauty of the site. Lieutenant de Bire pretended that the landscape resembled certain places in his beloved Pyrenees. Legoube described the area lyrically: "The clearing that climbs on both sides of the water creates in the dense and uniform forest a break that opens views toward distant peaks blue in the mists." For him, "going down to the river means not only getting water, washing up, doing my laundry or that of an immobilized comrade; going to the river also means nourishing my spirit with dreams and hope."

Those who, like Latanne, were lying on their cots, at least until they were able to move about, admired this luxuriant area when the sun chased away the last mists, after the rains stopped and the fog disappeared. They heard, more than they could see, the small monkeys making their noisy chatter.

Every officer realized that the presence among them of the French doctors, Gindrey and Premilieu, later Premilieu alone, giving them advice and rules of hygiene in place of the medicines they didn't have, contributed greatly to their survival. The noncommissioned officers and the soldiers did not have that privilege. Only one officer died in Tuan Giao, whereas among the other combatants mortality was very high. This officer death was painfully felt, as no one had expected it. Lieutenant Depoisier had been a strong person who never complained.

On a regular basis the Vietminh organized convoys on foot toward other hospital camps in Tonkin, described as paradises. In view of these journeys, Le Boudec and Datin volunteered to fetch the rice, about ten kilometers away. They wanted to exercise so they could better endure the long march from Tuan Giao to Tuyen Quang and, eventually, escape. They even cooked rice cakes to prepare for this presumed escape.

On June 11 a convoy of two hundred men, among whom were 11 officers and 160 wounded, left camp. Among the officers were Captains de Wilde and Hervouët, whom I knew well and had nursed in Dien Bien Phu. In transit they stayed in Tuan Giao only a few days. Hervouët had both feet and several wounds infected. He was not in great shape, but as did others, he carried on his back a young lieutenant of his group who had sprained his ankle. Exhausted and suffering from amoebic dysentery, Hervouët was first placed on a stretcher carried by de Wilde, Staff Sergeant Achard, and Chief Corporal Jansen, then dragged himself along to allow them to recuperate. He was set apart at each stop like a leper, showing exceptional dignity and courage. Hervouët died on July 10. De Wilde obtained permission from his captors to bury him according to our traditions and with military honor.

Captain Charles and Doctor Gindrey left Tuan Giao toward the end of June, determined to help each other at difficult times. Their column counted about a hundred disabled. The long march toward Camp No.1, near the Chinese border, started off: almost five hundred kilometers to walk in stages of twenty or twenty-five kilometers. "We have the luck to be alive, now we have to survive!" recalls Charles. To avoid being locked up in the mentality of prisoner-slaves, Charles and Gindrey decided to "think of themselves as reporters commissioned to study the logistics that allowed the Vietminh to win the battle." They also decided to respect certain rules of hygiene and diet and never to let themselves go. Before each meal they made themselves place under their rice bowl a square of parachute cloth as a tablecloth and then wash it every day.

The path was difficult, and despite the cast around his chest, Charles had to carry part of the salt ration for the column. He and Gindrey carried a man on a stretcher who was handicapped by an infected injury to his ankle. One night a Vietnamese prisoner slipped among them. He knew that he and his comrades would leave the convoy the next day, and he brought Charles a few opium pills against dysentery and a few other pills against malaria. A horrible fate awaited him if he was caught: being shot or having his Achilles' tendons slashed with a razor blade. A certain number of Vietnamese soldiers had endured this amputation and pulled themselves along on their elbows and knees, with insufficient food to survive, condemned to death in a few weeks, as Captain Cuq testified.

When Gindrey was exhausted, Charles carried his bag and encouraged him, and in return, when Charles slowed down from weakness, Gindrey was there to sustain him. "Comradeship, in the full sense of the word, is the best medicine," Charles later wrote.

One day, as rain was pouring down, the guards found shelter in a village and the prisoners were driven into a buffalo pen where, through the night, they were stung by insects and could not sleep.

Another time, during a halt, Charles went for his toilette near a creek bordered with reeds. He heard a noise and saw a young Tho woman who deposited two plates of food on the ground and then disappeared. He never forgot this comforting apparition.

Near the camps, the noncoms and the soldiers were directed toward one camp and Charles and Gindrey remained alone with their guards. They were lodged with the locals. One day they were staying with a former sharpshooter from the colonial period who was able to bring them food secretly, as his son had gone over to the Communist Party. It was heartwarming to know this man had not forgotten France. Soon they saw the straw huts of Camp No.1, where they rejoined their comrades and met those who had been there since October 1950, after the disasters of Cao Bang and Colonial Route 4.

On July 16 it was the turn of Le Boudec, Datin, Roux, Doctor Premilieu, Delobel, Carre, Bazin, Clement, Rollet, Lerain, Boulay, and other recaptured escapees, along with a few prisoners from the group Crèvecoeur, to leave their comrades from Tuan Giao by order of the Vietminh. They went with a sense of guilt at leaving behind those who still could not walk, but oh! with such a sense of relief at escaping that death camp. The group that departed on that day wore a piteous look. Those injured in the lungs panted and suffocated when the effort became too difficult. Roux, hit in the hip, limped along, leaning on a stick. He had no shoes and his feet were bleeding severely. Legrain limped also. Boulay, finally free from the ropes that had restrained him since his failed attempt to escape, was in better shape. Each man had to carry his own rice, and Le Boudec congratulated himself for having made a bag out of his old pants with a handmade needle.

The road was painful for the injured, even if the stages were "short": ten to fifteen kilometers. "Then we had to climb up to the pass of the Meos at night and under a beating rain, in total obscurity," recalls Le Boudec, "hours of dragging ourselves up, slipping back, falling, starting up again, sustaining those who threaten to give up and accept dying on the side of this rutted path." Crosses marked the graves of those who had died of exhaustion and were buried by their mates. The prisoners were savaged by the mosquitoes, the flies, and even the leeches. The march, though slow, was beyond the strength of bodies that had been underfed, were not in good physical shape, and whose morale was not always at its brightest.

Upon leaving Provincial Route 41, the group made its way toward Co Noi. The Black River was crossed under heavy guard because of the risk of escape. Going toward Yen Bay, some of the prisoners showed signs of utter exhaustion. Datin and Le Boudec hung back to help Major de Bazin. He wanted them to abandon him, but they carried him on their backs, each for a hundred yards. Next it was Le Boudec's turn to suffer from a fit of malaria. Datin, Roux, and Doctor Premilieu came to his aid and helped him to recover.

When the armistice was signed, the Vietminh did not announce it officially, but the prisoners were able to march by daylight, without fear of bombs.

On August 14 the convoy arrived at Tuyen Quang, then, after another day, at Camp No. 1. The nightmare was over, liberation was near. But not for everyone, unfortunately. Captain Desire, very ill, had been left behind at Tuyen Quang. Near him lay Sergeant Monchotte, in a coma, and they were both left to die. They probably would have died had not Major Tourret, passing through the camp, alerted the armistice commission in Vietri, which dispatched a helicopter.

At the same time the injured prisoners left at Tuan Giao were brought back to the Delta in Molotova trucks. However, as the camp was far from Route 41, all of them, including the worst off, had to reach the road on foot. Bailly, unable to walk, saw Viet soldiers set fire to his cot to force him to move. They saved him only at the last moment, and those severely wounded men at last rejoined their comrades.

It is well known that in all the cruel situations that face man, and even more when these situations are prolonged, the weak crack and the strong are revealed. After Dien Bien Phu, all was not pure heroism during the course of those long captivities. There were heroes and the selfish. If one admires the first, one must reserve judgment on those who gave in to the instinct to survive, confronted as they were by so much violence and by the despair of abandonment. Some who fell apart in captivity were able to recover their values, once their physical condition had been restored. Many of those who cracked were physically weaker, notably the younger ones, because it is only around the age of thirty that a man is in full possession of his faculties.

For all the prisoners who survived the long march and the infamy of the camps, it is very difficult, even after fifty years, to put these events behind. When one has fallen deeper than hell, how does one turn the page? How can one forget? And most of all, how does one distinguish, after the fact, the horror one feels at such human failings, at the perversity of certain torturers—while appreciating their poverty of means and those rare moments when some of them showed their humanity—from the ignominy of a system wholly devoted to degrading the weakest and to eliminating those who chose to resist it?

Memory, "this living mirror that makes us suffer every torture," as Maupassant said, often has great difficulty in sorting it all out.

Chapter Nine

HANOI-SAIGON-PARIS

Now I wish to return to the story of my own liberation. On May 24, 1954, after seventeen days of captivity at the hands of the Vietminh, I was free, Free but sad that I had to leave behind my comrades and my patients, for whom the hope of being liberated got dimmer by the day. I would so much have preferred leaving with the last ones.

In the little de Havilland Beaver that took me to Luang Prabang with Professor Huard, I listened closely to what he was saying to me: "I do not know if you realize that the whole world has its eyes on you, the only French woman in Dien Bien Phu, a prisoner of the Vietminh. Dozens of journalists and photographers await your arrival in Hanoi." I answered him: "So it seems the hardest part is not behind me." Nonetheless, I was happy in my freedom. I thought of my mother and my sister, whose anxiety was now over, and of my fellow flight nurses, whom I would rejoin in Hanoi.

The Beaver landed in Luang Prabang, where I received an extraordinary welcome. Its ambiance was wholly military, and friendly. It was a special moment that still warms my heart every time I think of it. As I descended from the plane, a detachment of Legionnaires presented arms. I was deeply touched as I passed before their ranks. They knew, of course, that on the anniversary of Camerone, Colonel Lemeunier had named me First Class of Honor of the Foreign Legion.

A young chief corporal asked me if I would like to telegraph my family, which I did immediately. Twenty-one years later, on the anniversary of Dien Bien Phu, I would receive a letter from that corporal, who served in the radio center in Luang Prabang:

I can still see you when you were liberated by the Vietminh on your arrival at the airport in Luang Prabang, on a beautiful afternoon of May 1954. I was there when you descended from the small Beaver. You had, I recall, put on the uniform of a paratrooper; you looked tired, somewhat lost after this incredible experience you had just lived, yet happy to have come back behind the French line. You felt very emotional, I believe, as you passed in review before the platoon of Legionnaires of the First Foreign Cavalry Regiment of paratroopers stationed in Luang Prabang who were presenting arms as you came down from the plane. It was very touching; everyone had eyes only for you and was proud to be honoring the young Frenchwoman.

Doctor Allehaut, attached to the French air force, came up to Doctor Huard and me, and I walked toward the medical unit while a young woman, probably a social assistant, offered me a refreshment. Under the tent of the unit, I rejoined my patients from Dien Bien Phu. They were waiting for their flight on the Dakotas, which would take them to Hanoi. The planes landed with two of my fellow flight nurses aboard: Elizabeth Gras and Chantal de Cotton. Our reunion was full of joy. After that first and short stop, I left for Hanoi with Chantal in the Dakota packed with the wounded. I had no idea of the crew's worries. Before landing in Luang Prabang they had to reconnoiter the area in hopes of spotting survivors from Dien Bien Phu. Unable to complete the refueling, the mechanic kept watching the fuel gage. For security reasons the major requested authorization to land in Bach Mai, one of Hanoi's two airports, closer than Gia Lam. This drew a crowd of officials, photographers, and reporters to welcome my arrival. As the plane came to a stop, it veered to the left and—suddenly—no more fuel! We were stuck on the taxiway until a tractor towed us back to the arrival site, where a large crowd awaited us.

It was nighttime, and as the door opened I was blinded by lightning and the camera flashes, and I could not help stepping back. At the foot of the stairs stood General Cogny, commander of the land forces of North Vietnam, General Dechaux, commander of the air force in Tonkin, and a third officer, Captain Jean de Heaulme, provisionally detached from his group of airborne commandos to take part in the dealings to exchange prisoners. Two years later, this young captain with whom I shared a distant parentage would become my husband, but that idea did not cross either of our minds at the time.

I was very touched by the warmth of General Cogny's welcome. To protect me from the journalists, who had set siege to the flight nurses' house, General Dechaux offered me refuge in his hotel, which served as the headquarters for Air Command. For many years this great-hearted graduate of the École Polytechnique, a true nobleman, a man of style and of conviction, had acted as a faithful supporter of the flight nurses, always available when any of us needed his help. When one of us was shot in the lung inside a Dakota hit by Vietminh antiaircraft, the general went to the hospital to share with her a package he had just received, full of products from Auvergne, succulent and impossible to find here—a small gesture from a generous heart.

During the few days I spent at the hotel, General Dechaux acted toward me as a real father. On the evening of my arrival he invited to dinner all the flight nurses from the northern detachment, a heart-warming evening. But in all our thoughts were those who remained in Dien Bien Phu: Doctor Grauwin, the medical personnel, and the captured wounded who would be taken to the Viet camps regardless of their condition. The general had the sensitivity to invite my promotion classmate, Alberte Othnin-Girard, to stay with me so that I would not feel alone. We had so much to talk about.

The next day General Dechaux accompanied me to a press conference organized by Captain Gerard de Lassus, press officer for General Cogny, to answer the eager questions of reporters from all nationalities and those of the men's families. I was counseled not to discuss the conditions of their detention so as to avoid interfering with the ongoing negotiations for their liberation. I have reviewed the films of that conference. They reflect indeed the immense sadness that strangled me as I spoke of the wounded, and the fear I had of saying something that could be badly misinterpreted or taken out of context and cause harm to my prisoner comrades.

I kept being asked the same two questions: "Were you scared in Dien Bien Phu? Were you afraid to die?" I don't believe I was scared during the fighting, even during the most violent and endless shelling. But I was frightened the night of May 7 when I found myself alone, for what seemed an eternity, before the Vietminh political commissar and the camp commandant. I also felt a chill when the Viets wanted me to live with the young Vietnamese women because they found it inappropriate for a woman to live among men.

As far as a fear of death goes, I didn't think of it. I had a very strong conviction that all risks were assumed and necessary to evacuate, care for, and save the injured. My faith certainly helped, even if it was not as reflective or as deep as it is today. Being Catholic and believing in eternal life, I see death not as an end in itself but as a passage to a real life.

The press conference, organized to avoid the assaults of the journalists, did not prevent Lucien Bodard, war correspondent for *France-Soir*, from pursuing me and, after I refused an interview, writing a headline: "The Shadow of the Vietminh Hovers over Geneviève de Galard." At that time I was still traumatized for having been forced to write to Ho Chi Minh, and the comment hurt.

Soon after, I returned to France, but I could not leave Hanoi without going to Lanessan Hospital to visit my patients. I telephoned Colonel Nicot, who commanded Air Transport, and he agreed to delay my departure by forty-eight hours. During my visits I was accompanied by Captain de Heaulme, who in his function in the negotiations with the Vietminh interviewed the wounded on the conditions of their detention and their liberation.

In Saigon I received another warm welcome, this time from General Lauzun, chief of the air force in Indochina, and from Madame Lauzun, Colonel Nicot, and my cousin Colonel de Vulpillières, who pinned on me the Legion of Honor earned by my uncle, Colonel de Franclieu, a great wounded veteran who had hoped it would reach me in Dien Bien Phu. Then I went to Grall Hospital, where I found some of my former patients, such as Simon Marie, the blinded nineteen year old. Immediately he recognized my voice. To thank me for what I had done for him in Dien Bien Phu, he picked up his harmonica and said, "Listen, Geneviève, I've composed this tune for you."

I also wanted to go to the rest center in Dalat to visit, in particular, Lieutenant Rondeau, who had been wounded in the abdomen, had almost died on two occasions, and had been among the last liberated. It turned out to be impossible and when I learned, shortly after, of his death due to complications, I felt terribly sad. I kept imagining how his widowed mother, with the loss of her only son just as she waited for his return home, must have felt.

The day of my return to Paris, the journalists attacked once more. In the crowd I recognized Major Edouard Bonhour, the husband of a friend of my sister, whom I knew well. I ran up to him and begged him to stay by my side—and a reporter wrote that the army had assigned a bodyguard to prevent me from speaking! My friend's presence helped a great deal because I was not feeling up to par. Besides suffering from a seven-headed anthrax in Dien Bien Phu, my legs were still swollen from beriberi. My run-down condition caused a boil to appear on my arm. During the flight, the altitude and the changes in pressure gave the staph infection a chance to spread in my whole arm; the swelling increased hour by hour. It was totally compressed in the sleeve of my uniform when the plane landed in Paris-Orly, after several stops, on that June 1.

My mother was waiting at the airport, moved to tears, as I was. My uncle, Raymond de Galard, our guardian since my father's death, accompanied her. Guite de Guyencourt, our chief flight nurse, also was there, as well as Marie-Rose Calmettes, the childhood friend through whom I discovered the corps of flight nurses. Dozens of photographers were present, but I did not see them. I suddenly found myself confronted by a popularity that I neither wanted nor sought. It felt quite unreal. But I was wonderfully happy when a journalist informed us that Doctor Grauwin and the personnel of the medical units had been liberated. Having no news, I thought of them so often, fearing that they might be in one of those terrible camps where so many of our combatants were to die.

My uncle drove us to his daughter's house in Versailles, where I was surrounded by reporters and photographers who wanted an interview at all cost. I refused, and in the next morning's paper they quoted me as saying to the wives of the prisoners, crowded before the door, "Have pity, I am exhausted." It was from the reporters' insistence that I was trying to protect myself, not from those anxious women!

To escape the press, we concocted a few subterfuges. Taking us out through the garden gate, my uncle drove us to his wife's property, where I spent a week sheltered from the reporters. Thanks to the antibiotics and compresses that my mother and my aunt kept applying, all risk of septicemia disappeared. This was fortunate because I faced a merry-go-round of official obligations at the Ministry of Veterans and at the Air Ministry's military salute, where Monsieur Christiaens, the minister, presented me the medal of aeronautics. On that occasion I was surrounded by my comrades, and their affectionate presence helped a lot. A few days after my liberation, Madame Christiaens planned to visit the wounded in Percy Hospital and I was invited to join her, along with Guite de Guyencourt, our chief. How happy I was to find Captain Cabiro there, nicknamed "the Cab," a heroic figure among the paratroopers.

That same week I received a letter signed by Captain Hélie de Saint Marc, whom at the time I did not know, and by five other young officers from the 11th BPC. Mailed from Perpignan on June 3, 1954, it read, "From the officers of the 11th Paratrooper Battalion to Mademoiselle Geneviève de Galard: You will never know how much we thought of you and your comrades during the terrible days you spent in Dien Bien Phu. You represented for us devotion and ultimate abnegation of self. We ask that you leave us with this impression. You can no longer allow yourself to be a woman like all the others. Forget all propaganda and publicity. Our comrades do not require magazine articles or movies. History will judge them, you were with them, that is enough."

I read this letter as an homage. Yet its fraternal advice was not necessary: It was not in my nature to profit from the suffering of my patients or to seek glory and honor. If later I happened to recall and speak about the past, it was always to help out those who had asked me to.

In Dien Bien Phu, Colonel Langlais had told me of the offer from a large American news agency that promised a mountain of gold for an exclusive on my recollections. Back in Paris I was again solicited by the Americans, this time to ask for my consent for a movie; my role was to be played by Leslie Caron. But my answer was negative.

One of the first tasks I undertook in France was to answer the letters sent me by the families of those still in Indochina. Every day a wave of letters arrived in Coëtquidan, where my sister, Marie-Suzanne, had taken me in. In order to answer all this mail, our chief granted me one month of leave, from June 15 to July 15. It was not exactly a vacation: I dedicated twelve to fourteen hours a day to answering all the letters, and I did not have a minute to myself. The prisoners' families, mad with anxiety, expected so much from me, hoping that I would remember their sons, their husbands, or their brothers. In some cases I did remember. But often there was a world of difference between the shaven and neat faces I discovered in the photos and those of the wounded that I had taken in, covered in mud, or that I had nursed and followed after they had been operated on in our unit.

Chapter Ten

TRIUMPH ON BROADWAY

O n July 26, 1954, two months after my return from Dien
Bien Phu, I suddenly landed in another world. Seated on the
back of a superb black Cadillac that progressed up Broadway at a walker's pace, tightly hugging a bouquet in my left arm, dressed
in my white flight nurse uniform and navy blue beret, I waved with my
right hand to the multitude of New Yorkers who welcomed me. We were
surrounded by marching bands. A rain of confetti and multicolored bal-
loons fell from the adjacent buildings. The sidewalks were crowded with
people; office employees were leaning out of windows waving their arms
at us. From all sides I could hear clapping and enthusiastic whistles.

A few exclamations reached me as in a dream: "Vive la France,"
"Bravo!" and even "Vive Geneviève!" The warmth of the New Yorkers'
reception left me speechless. Unperturbed, the long automobile, flying
both the star-spangled banner and the French tricolor, pursued its majestic progress at the bottom of the cold cement canyons of Manhattan. At
that moment I felt a sort of split within myself. I became a spectator of
this incredible event: The people of the New World were offering to the
little French nurse of Dien Bien Phu the traditional celebration reserved
for those they wanted to welcome as heroes! I was experiencing what
Americans call a "ticker-tape parade." At the time the American newspa-
pers reported it as the noisiest ticker-tape parade since that held in 1926
for Gertrude Ederle after she swam the English Channel.

Seated near me in the car, wearing white gloves and a small, dark
straw hat with an egret feather, was Frances Bolton, a Republican congresswoman, a radiant, energetic, and decisive woman whom I had only

met that morning at the airport but who was the cause of my presence on American soil. On June 25 she had presented to Congress the following resolution: "Congress offers to Mlle de Galard Terraube their warmest felicitations for her conduct in Dien Bien Phu and invites her, in the name of the American government, to come to the United States" for the centenary of Florence Nightingale's nursing of the wounded in the Crimean War. The British nurse had organized field hospitals, not only in the Near East but also during the American Civil War and the Franco-Prussian War of 1870, and had organized training for all hospital workers.

According to the American press, that was the first time since the visit of Marquis de Lafayette in 1821 that a foreign citizen had been invited by an act of Congress to come to the United States on an official visit. At that time the United States had even sent a ship to bring back the French hero of the American Revolution. Another invitation of this kind had been extended in 1851 to the Hungarian patriot Louis Kossuth, who had played an important role in the Hungarian revolution of 1848, but never had such an honor been offered to a woman.

To tell the truth this invitation to spend three weeks in the United States, so spectacular and so soon after my liberation, left me feeling overwhelmed. When, in Paris, the minister of air told me of it, my first reaction was to decline, even though the invitation had enclosed a gracious letter signed by President Eisenhower, who seemed to consider my acceptance as certain:

Dear Mademoiselle de Galard Terraube,

It is with great pleasure that I send you a resolution from the Congress of the United States inviting you, as soon as it may be convenient for you and for your country, to come visit the United States as a guest of honor.

The people of the United States have followed with sympathy and profound admiration the courageous and determined resistance by the forces of the French Union to the communist aggression. I want to be among all those who have found the example given by your courage, your devotion to duty, and your concern for the sick and for the wounded, as edifying and in accordance with the finest traditions of humanity.

Dwight D. Eisenhower

What was I to answer? I felt very awkward being offered these honors when I had only done what I was expected to do and when many of my comrades were still rotting in those hellish camps, under constant psychological pressures from their captors. A cousin of mine, Louis de Guiringaud, who was consul for France in San Francisco, helped me change my mind. "Geneviève, you must go," he insisted while on a visit to Paris. So I decided to accept, partly out of obedience and partly out of duty, what I considered a mission for the cause of France. I was told that Congress wanted me to come for the Fourth of July celebrations or, if impossible, then on July 12, in time for festivities being prepared to celebrate July 14, our Bastille Day, but I absolutely could not make it.

Under the circumstances there was no way I was going to take part in such grandiose festivities. I responded that I wished the character of my trip to maintain its appropriate simplicity and dignity. Also, I could not leave France before accomplishing my other duty, even more important to me: to answer every family who had written me for news of a loved one, injured and still prisoner or lost in the conflicts.

My departure was finally set for July 25, and it raised a question that any young woman would ask herself: What shall I wear? During the day it was simple. I would wear a full-dress flight nurse uniform: a white suit to substitute for our everyday uniform and the navy blue beret I sported everywhere. But what about the many receptions I had to attend in the evenings?

Colonel de Bordas, now a general, who sensed my dilemma, came providentially to my aid. Thanks to one of his friends from the air force, who now worked with Jacques Fath, I was put in touch with the great couturier. Fath agreed to design a cocktail outfit and an evening dress for me, and—something one could hardly imagine today—he did not want me to publicize him by letting it be known who had created the clothes. He only wanted to offer a special homage, through his talents, to the French forces. His name was never mentioned in the American press. I imposed the same conditions on the person who served as our intermediary.

Jacques Fath helped me choose the fabrics, the styles, and patterns. He put his whole heart into it, taking the time to attend the fittings in his salon. The cocktail ensemble was made of champagne-colored shantung; the evening dress was in gray organza with white dots, very full, very *décolleté,* with a facing of white organdy and a belt with two panels of sky blue satin.

In the Air France Constellation that carried me to the United States I had all the time in the world to analyze the possible reasons why Congress should have sent me this prestigious and astonishing invitation. The official reason was obviously to render to the combatants of Dien Bien Phu the homage of the American people, and I was determined to show that, through me, this homage could only be offered to them, as well as to the flight nurses and medical personnel who dedicated themselves to their care in the planes and the hospitals.

Certain members of Congress, among them Mrs. Bolton, certainly regretted that American assistance had not been greater to help the besieged garrison of Dien Bien Phu. Was inviting me to visit their country a way to assuage their consciences? Several months earlier the United States had been prepared to increase its aid, but it wanted the British to join in that effort. Faced with a refusal from London, Washington had abstained. During the siege of Dien Bien Phu I could not indulge in this sort of political reflection, as I was obviously not up to date as to what was being considered. I would hear some of the men wonder if bombs could not be dropped on the Communists' rear positions, if the Americans decided to do so. Some even spoke of an atomic bomb, but I considered those thoughts fantasies.

Was Congress also hoping, through this invitation, to sensitize the American people to the situation on the Indochinese peninsula, where they would later choose to intervene? But the Geneva Conference had only ended on July 21, so this interpretation was perhaps somewhat premature.

Once on American territory I would learn through the press that other considerations, more political, were at work. A newswoman from the *Washington Post* explained that my visit would have the merit of sensitizing the people in the United States to the country's need for nurses. Mrs. Bolton would later confirm this interpretation on a television appearance. Besides, to the younger generations, I was supposed to incarnate the value of service to others and a sense of duty. The entire American press would soon be comparing me to Florence Nightingale walking among the dead and the wounded in Crimea. It is a surprising country that always has the need in the middle of triumphant materialism to call upon great moral principles.

My arrival in New York on Monday July 26, shortly before 9:00 AM, was unforgettable. The mayor, Robert F. Wagner, took the trouble to meet me. Two hundred people were waiting for me in front of Hangar 7 at Idlewild Airport and started clapping when I, bursting with emotion, stepped on the platform of the ramp, ready to give a small speech in response to the official declarations of welcome. Mrs. Bolton, who spoke French very well, presented me to the press as a "symbol of free world femininity and of the great heroic deeds of the nursing profession." She even portrayed me as a symbol of the courage of women in the fight by the free world against communism. To add to my anxiety, Roger Seydoux, plenipotentiary minister at the French embassy, came aboard, even before I emerged from the plane, to inform me of a recent event about which the reporters were likely to question me. They were going to ask me to comment on international politics, on matters way above my head. I did not want to fail in my role or say anything that, misinterpreted, could harm the interests of my comrades still in captivity. I was haunted by that thought.

"I haven't earned this honor, because I only did my duty." Having learned them by heart before leaving Paris, those words in English helped to loosen my throat, and I managed to add, as I held on tightly to the bouquet of red roses and white carnations given to me on landing, "This honor is offered, through me, to all those whose lives I was proud to share in Dien Bien Phu and to all the nurses who devote themselves to lessen the sufferings of the injured. My thoughts, at this moment, are with all those who are still over there and who, far more than I, have earned this honor that you offer. I think also of all their families."

As soon as I finished, a journalist asked me the first question about my opinion of the present truce in Indochina. Mrs. Bolton sharply interrupted him: "No politics, please." When the journalist insisted, I attempted a prudent response: "Peace had to intervene to stop this human hemorrhage." I quickly added, "I haven't read the papers these past few days." An American newspaper nevertheless concluded that I did not hesitate to discuss political matters—despite all the efforts of my hosts to protect me. Later I had to explain that my title of lieutenant is purely honorary and that I did not want to be addressed as lieutenant.

When I was asked about my two letters to Ho Chi Minh, I gave a cautious and prepared answer, knowing that the international press had already published interpretations influenced by Vietminh propaganda. At least as I see it, the letter I had to write on the occasion of Ho Chi Minh's birthday was that of a nurse focused on helping the injured whose evacuation was becoming more urgent every day. I reminded the reporter of the second letter of thanks for my liberation—a gesture of courtesy that seemed to me necessary—in which I asked for the freedom of the French doctors and medics who had stayed with me in Dien Bien Phu to care for the wounded.

My first test by the American press did not go too badly. The reporters started calling me the "Angel of Dien Bien Phu," although never in the camp had it remotely occurred to anyone to tag me with that ethereal moniker. The journalists teased me kindly for my accent, saying that I use *z* in place of *th*. They wrote feelingly of my shy smile, my dimples, my cheeks pink and round, and the freckles on my forehead. To them I became the "little brunette" or even "sweet Geneviève" or simply "Jennie." The *New York Times* affirmed that I did not look at all as having been involved in a fifty-seven-day siege but that I looked more like the "French cousin" any American would be proud to claim for his own.

After this first press conference I was whisked off in the majestic Cadillac, in a flurry of cars and roaring motorcycles, to the parade on Broadway, through a crowd of 250,000 New Yorkers, and to City Hall. There I was touched once more by the kind words of Robert Wagner: "Your heroism, your bravery and your noble heart have conquered the imagination and hearts of all our people; you have given a great example of love and devotion. You are not only the heroine of Dien Bien Phu, but also of the free world. This city, New York, the capital of the world, is now your city because you are truly a Lady of the World." I answered in a tiny voice, choked by emotion and barely audible, to the two thousand people assembled in the park at City Hall. After the national anthem and the reception, I was driven to the Plaza Hotel along Lafayette Avenue, Park Avenue, and Fifth Avenue, the route the parade of cars followed from Thirty-fourth Street to Fifty-ninth Street; it had been extended to Fifth Avenue to allow a greater number of New Yorkers to greet me.

Before dinner with the French consul, Jean de Lagarde, in midafternoon I attended a cocktail party hosted by Frances Bolton, during which several nursing associations presented me with decorations, among them the medal of Florence Nightingale, and one decoration from Columbia University. From all sides I was asked for a word, a signature, a dedication on a photograph. The nurses' associations had the sensitivity to invite a young French veteran to this event, wounded in 1951 during the

Korean War. Paralyzed from the waist to the feet, he had been attending a reeducation program in New York. Throughout my wanderings in the States, during all my visits to hospitals and nursing schools, I was irresistibly drawn by these wounded for life, these amputees or blinded veterans whose path I crossed for a few moments. They reminded me so much, in their eyes, in every detail of their limbs and flesh, of "my" wounded of Dien Bien Phu.

On July 27 I flew to Washington, D.C., in a U.S. Air Force C-47 for a three-day stay. There a new official welcome awaited me. In a symbolic homage, at the airport I was given the keys to the city. A hundred people stood in the torrid heat, and the U.S. Air Force Band played both the Marseillaise and the American national anthem. Henri Bonnet, the French ambassador, and his wife were there to welcome me, as were the Norwegian ambassador, a senior member of the diplomatic corps, two members of the House Foreign Affairs Committee, and officials from the State Department. Two particularly moving events awaited me in the capital.

As I entered the Capitol Building through the visitors' corridor, all members of the House stood to greet me with their applause. It was totally unexpected and even against the rules. I was on my way, in fact, to lunch with members of the House in the Speaker's dining room, and I had only peeked in to see the House gallery. By a strange coincidence, at that same moment a debate was taking place over a proposition to reduce military aid in Indochina. Having noticed my unexpected entrance, a representative from Minnesota, Republican Walter Judd, tried to draw his colleagues' attention to me. But the presiding member banged his gavel to remind the assembly that it was forbidden to signal the presence of visitors. Walter Judd responded that he only wished to "welcome to this country the Angel of Dien Bien Phu, wherever she may be." This subterfuge set off peals of laughter among the attendants, who applauded as they turned toward me.

The other unforgettable moment occurred on the terrace of the White House. President Eisenhower pinned on me the Medal of Freedom, the highest American distinction, in front of his wife, Mamie, who was very popular in the United States; Mrs. Bolton; and Ambassador Bonnet. The Medal of Freedom can only be given by the president of the United States; the secretary of state, equivalent to the French minister of foreign affairs; or the secretaries of defense, navy, air force, or army. It was awarded for outstanding service for the peace and the security of the United States beyond the borders of the nation. The president introduced me as the "woman of the year." Despite the grandmotherly attentions of Mamie and the smiling efforts of the famous Ike to put me at ease, I still felt very intimidated.

Later my visit to Arlington Cemetery, and particularly to the Nurses' Memorial, left me with a profound impression. It was my first visit to a military cemetery and I found that the place exuded an exceptional sense of serenity and beauty. How could I help but think of all the dead in Dien Bien Phu who, in those last days, could not receive the burial they had merited?

Since my arrival in the United States, three American nurses had been escorting me: one from the U.S. Navy, with whom I corresponded until her death a few years ago, one from the U.S. Air Force, and one from the U.S. Army. With them I visited Walter Reed Army Medical Center, where I met many paraplegics. That evening Ambassador Bonnet warmly greeted me at the French embassy, where a reception was held in my honor. I was pleased when he introduced me to Vice President and Mrs. Richard Nixon.

Throughout this long journey, the private secretary of Louis de Guiringaud, Michele Couturier, followed my every step. My cousin in San Francisco had generously offered to do without her for three weeks so that I never had to feel alone, I had a constant French presence, and I could ask her for the American words I couldn't remember. I highly appreciated her help, especially when I learned that an official trip was an exhausting marathon. Endlessly I had to sign a dedication, pronounce a few thanks, attend a new reception. Everywhere I went I was treated as a princess and housed in the best hotels; my rooms were always decorated with flowers, and I was offered the assistance of a hairdresser. What a contrast to the weeks I had just lived. All those receptions, all that luxury almost appeared indecent. But I had not asked for them and I refused to feel guilty; in any case it was not in my nature to do so. I even lived those moments with a certain joy.

I wrote to my mother, commenting on my impressions: "The welcome of the Americans is touching. I had difficulty in France imagining how they had followed the battle of Dien Bien Phu. I am getting a lot of very moving accounts. Everyone tries to do something nice for me. Very kindly, they ask if there are places I would like to go to, what I would like to add to the program." Thus I asked to visit the flight nurses' school where one of us, Michaela de Clermont-Tonnerre, had spent a month in training. I was able to visit my aunt, Caroline de Galard, a sister of St. Vincent and my father's first cousin. I could also visit Madame Langlais, the mother of Colonel Langlais, who was still prisoner in Indochina. She happened to be in the United States, visiting her daughter, who was married to an American; she was anxious and thirsty for news and I was happy to speak to her about her son. Later, in September, after his liberation, Colonel Langlais would write from Saigon to thank me for "the great joy and profound emotion" his mother and sister felt at my visit.

From Washington my journey continued on course on July 30 to Cleveland, where I was received by mounted police and an official escort. There again I was solemnly offered the keys to the city. This three-day stop in the state Mrs. Bolton represented in Congress allowed me to know her strong personality better.

In Cleveland I was welcomed by her son and daughter-in-law, who entertained me for the weekend in a family atmosphere that I truly appreciated after all those days of official receptions and press conferences, during which I always worried about not measuring up. Nonetheless my hosts organized in my honor a magnificent reception for three thousand people, bringing together every notable in the city in their splendid white house in the middle of a park shaded by hundred-year-old trees. Some children brought me bouquets of flowers. They were very shy, as I was at the age of seven when I had to greet my mother's guests. After dinner, served on small tables in the garden, for desert the pièce de résistance was an enormous cake in the shape of the Arc de Triomphe!

On August 1, at the end of a performance in an outdoor theater, a mini "coup de théâtre" occurred that typified the whole atmosphere of my trip. The actress who played the heroine handed me the bouquet of roses she had just received. Everyone in the audience rose for an enthusiastic ovation that lasted at least five minutes.

From August 3 to 6 my trip extended to Chicago for a visit devoted to the important medical centers of the city, in particular the Veterans Hospital, where I met with the doctors and medics from the various departments. They gave me a parchment signed by nearly every patient, all veterans of the wars fought since 1899.

After a stop in Denver I spent a second weekend of relaxation at Lake Tahoe, in a magnificent setting of giant sequoias. Someone offered to take me water skiing on the icy waters of the lake, situated at six thousand feet. I had never water skied and I was eager to try it. After two unsuccessful attempts, not wanting to give up despite the cold, I tried again, and this time I took off for an unbelievably thrilling tour.

The next stop was San Francisco. On my visit of this beautiful city, built on steep hills connected by cable cars to the flat areas near the harbor, I discovered the famous Golden Gate Bridge. After a visit to a hospital, lunch at the headquarters of the Red Cross, and cocktails hosted by the French colony, my cousin, Louis de Guiringaud, consul of France, hosted a dinner for me with a few friends.

In Dallas, during a short stop at the airport, a small ceremony had been organized at which I was given a diploma attesting that I am "qualified to wear a Stetson and spurs on my boots." I was then given a beautiful king-sized Texas sombrero, which delighted the photographers, always on alert for a good photo-op.

New Orleans captured me with its charm, its pretty wooden houses in the French colonial style, and its nightclubs where I could listen to African American music, which enchanted me. There also I was given a key to the city—very small, a real jewel—and I was made a "citizen of honor" of this ancient city, the old capital of French Louisiana, where the memory of my country to this day remains very alive.

On our return to New York, a detour that would allow me to fly over and discover the Grand Canyon, one of the marvels of our planet, was arranged. That unbelievable journey ended with a last stop in New York before flying home to France. During a High Mass at St. Patrick's Cathedral on Fifth Avenue, Monsignor Flanders, auxiliary bishop of New York, welcomed me from his pulpit in such elegiac terms that he made me blush.

That same day I was invited for lunch at the residence of Cardinal Spellman, archbishop of New York, who handed me his personal medal. The speech he gave after lunch was a testimony of admiration and sympathy addressed, through me, to every combatant of Dien Bien Phu. He was a considerable personality, a major figure of American Catholicism. A friend of Pope Pius XII, Cardinal Spellman had been at the center of the first sustained dialogue between the United States and the Holy See and had been described as a sincere nationalist, an astute political prelate.

During a stay in Paris on May 20, 1954, Cardinal Spellman uttered these words: "Nowadays, at Dien Bien Phu, a new 'Song of Roland' epic has been written. The horn of Roland that, twelve centuries ago, sounded in the pass of Roncevaux and recalled to battle the men of Charlemagne, rang out again on the plateau of Dien Bien Phu. On hearing this clarion call, inviting free men throughout the world to waken, and to show the same spirit as these few heroes who, from the ashes of defeat, rekindled the flames of hope, our soul was deeply stirred." And though at that time I was still a prisoner, he even mentioned my actions, going as far as to say that I had shown myself worthy "to take [her] place in that line of French women who had shared the glory of Jeanne d'Arc." Such words demonstrated the impact that the events at Dien Bien Phu had on the American world.

It was with my meeting with that amazing personage that my three weeks on the American continent came to an end.

Chapter Eleven

ALWAYS A FLIGHT NURSE

After my visit to the United States I returned to Paris, where I was besieged again with myriad solicitations. Sometimes I was sorry to disappoint, but I did not see myself as a full-time conference speaker. Luckily my contract with the French air force had not expired and I could reenter the ranks and take up my work as a flight nurse.

Yet my life had changed. I used every moment of free time to go to the Val-de-Grâce Hospital to visit the wounded that had been liberated. And for a while I continued to be the unwilling prey of journalists. One day, as I drove around the streets of Paris, I was literally chased by them. I stopped by a policeman, lowered my window, and begged him to help me. He ordered me to park on the side as he waved the pursuing car past me. The street was one-way and I was safe.

But I felt that my life was split between before and after Dien Bien Phu.

My leave had been spent writing letters, and the official trip to the United States had been very tiring, so I took some time to rest in the Gers, to the southwest, above the Pyrenees, where my father's youngest brother lived. Thus I missed the return to Paris of the Dien Bien Phu combatants, liberated from Viet Tri and Sam Son in late August and early September, because of the accords in Geneva. Madame Bigeard had the sensitivity to let me know on what day her husband was arriving in Paris, and I regretted not being there, but it was natural that he should have time to catch up with his wife and daughter. That would not prevent us meeting later in a restaurant on the Champs-Élysées, however, where the signs of sympathy from those who recognized us warmed our hearts. Fortunately I was back in time to meet at Paris-Orly Airport the wounded, who were repatriated via the United States on American Globemasters. On board were a flight nurse and convoy nurse.

Our chief, Guite de Guyencourt, did not want to send me back to Indochina. She preferred that I have no contact with the Vietminh. But my fellow nurses were now involved in a mission in North Vietnam to evacuate the thousands of Vietnamese who did not want to live under a Communist regime. France was bringing to what was now being called South Vietnam, by plane and ship, those who preferred exile to the loss of their religious freedom.

In November 1954 I was allowed a round-trip flight to Saigon to convoy troops on board the Sky (DC6 Skymaster). Despite all that I had endured in Dien Bien Phu, I was really pleased to come back to this captivating country. At Tan Son Nhut, Saigon's airport, I was greeted by Solange de Peyerimhoff, a flight nurse I was very fond of, who told me of her missions in North Vietnam. Later I joyfully embraced Doctor Gindrey and his wife, a nurse in Saigon.

For the first anniversary of Operation Castor, I was happy to be back in France, at Bayonne, where a ceremony took place for the dead of Dien Bien Phu. In front of the monument an immense tricolor flag was displayed, held at the corners by Colonel Langlais, Lieutenant Colonel Bigeard, Major Bazin de Bezons, and Major Tourret. What joy I felt to stand again with them.

In February 1955 I was granted time for a ski holiday in Mirabel, in a chalet reserved for the flying personnel of the French air force. The first few evenings I fell asleep at 8:30 PM. After three days, I felt radiant with health and energy for the first time since my return from Dien Bien Phu. I had been dragging myself on my missions, unable to recuperate from the exhaustion of Dien Bien Phu and the trip to the United States, but now I was in full form to leave again for two months in Algiers to work on the Sahara flights. I still remember, on one of those missions, the extraordinary reception from the Foreign Legion in Sebha, where a mechanical problem on our plane allowed us to stay over twenty-four hours. First the officers, then the noncommissioned officers, sang the Legion's traditional song. About thirty of them who had been in Dien Bien Phu invited me to have a drink with them before lunch. And on Sunday afternoon, the officers took me on a long tour around the base with four cars going full speed on the sand trails. I loved it!

On my return from Algiers to France I was given the mission to accompany the French basketball team to the Special Paraplegics Olympics in Stokemandeville, England. It was at my request that the air force lent us the plane. Seeing these men play basketball in their wheelchairs inspired such admiration for their courage, dynamism, and joy at being alive. I understood that day how much sports can contribute to the handicapped's reeducation and reinsertion into the everyday world. In France the handicapped owe much to a veteran of World War II, Philippe Berthé, an amputee of one leg who founded the Sport Association of French Handicapped, which later became the Handisport Federation.

Vietnam called me again in May 1955, but only south of the seventeenth parallel. Since the accords in Geneva, North Vietnam had been in the hands of the Vietminh. My normal missions were now Saigon-Tourane (Da Nang) or Saigon–Bien Hoa–Tourane, Saigon-Vientiane. We still had medical missions, most often for people injured by mines. But our lives as flight nurses no longer had anything to do with our lives as flight nurses in 1953–54. Our days off, on Sundays, gave us a chance to explore the areas around Saigon. On the way to visit my brother-in-law, Christian de Villepin, attached to the 1st Chasseurs, I was struck by the vast number of churches on the road to Bien Hoa. Catholics from North Vietnam had settled there, and the first thing they had done was to build a church, as lovely as possible, thus expressing their faith. They had left all they possessed in North Vietnam in order to continue to live it, and I was full of admiration for these people who, in the course of three generations, had been martyred for their beliefs.

Saigon had not really changed. In comparison to Hanoi, which was more provincial and more intimate, with its shaded avenues and the charm of its Petit Lac, Saigon was very lively, particularly Cholon, its Chinatown, where I enjoyed spending time. In 1954 I had not been very attracted to South Vietnam. Saigon appeared irrelevant when so much was going on to the north, even when one day I went with my crew to visit an opium den. We knew nothing of the surrounding Cochinchina outside of Saigon. But on my visits to my cousin in An Loc, he took me to see the beautiful rubber plantations and the factory that treated the latex to transform it into rubber. I marveled at the lovely scenery around

Cap St. Jacques (Vung Tau). In truth it was the first time I had ever seen a peaceful Vietnam, and I filled my eyes and heart with all its beauty.

As my flight schedule reminded me, I was traveling a lot those days, sometimes to accompany troops but other times on a medical mission that brought back the past. One day I had the joy of running into Doctor Grauwin. Together we visited the Vietnamese amputees who had been wounded and operated on in Dien Bien Phu. We found them almost abandoned; some had not yet even received their citations of merit. For them Grauwin was their savior. Between two flights I went back to see them and brought them cigarettes.

One day I was appointed to fly to Angkor, Cambodia, with a team of researchers who were going there to observe a total eclipse of the sun. The aircraft was loaded with sophisticated instruments and a few passengers, all scientists. With the crew I visited the great temples Angkor Thom and Angkor Vat, then we went on toward Bantai Shrei. After miles in a jeep on incredibly bumpy trails, suddenly, in the middle of the jungle, a marvel of beauty appeared, graceful and elegant with its sculptures of Apsara and Naja. At the moment we visited Tap Rom temple the eclipse occurred and the sun disappeared. Darkness covered the stone split by thick roots; the effect was extraordinary, almost Dantesque. One of my dreams had just come true—to see Angkor, its splendor.

The days were going by fast, and I started to realize how sad I was at the idea of having to leave this country again so soon, as my contract with the air force would expire on July 15, 1955.

Back in France I received a letter from General Cogny that touched me deeply: Before leaving Tonkin, he wanted to tell me that he had a special thought of me—on this first anniversary of the end of the combat in Dien Bien Phu. How time speeds by. One year already.

Retrospectively I lamented the immense waste this war in Vietnam represented, as I hoped that the people we had learned to love would arrive one day at true freedom in independence. Much blood had flowed; we had mixed our blood with theirs in what was their civil war, and those years of sharing were a guarantee of hope for the future of our friendship.

Chapter Twelve

REMAINING FAITHFUL

S ome of my comrades, on their return from the hell of the camps, and after that of Dien Bien Phu, wanted to turn a new page in their lives. Personally I could not do that. I felt joined to all my comrades by everlasting ties. We had shared too much suffering. I felt a sort of debt toward them, toward the families of those who had given their lives or their physical integrity when I had the luck to come out of it without a scratch.

But what was I going to do now? How was I to remain faithful to those exceptional moments that I had been given to share? How could I keep myself from becoming anesthetized little by little by the soft and comfortable life that I could easily slip into back in France? "One must live in revolt," said Albert Camus. How could I keep from disappointing those who, with Hélie de Saint Marc in June 1954, had written me, "You have represented for us devotion and abnegation to the ultimate limit. You can no longer allow yourself to be a woman like all the others"?

This duty obsessed me, and I often would think back to the answer I had given to Professor Huard when he had warned me of the media's pressure that awaited me in Hanoi: "I think that the hardest part is not behind me." It seemed to me harder to live nobly the monotonous course of daily life than to live those exceptional moments when we had been carried along by exultation and solidarity. Gradually I discovered the truth of Jacques d'Arnoux's words in the epigraph to this book: "Heroism lies less in the nature of acts than in the manner they are accomplished." And I understood that the simplest actions of life could be enriched if done out of love.

Events helped me find my path. A few months after the end of my contract with the French air force I met an American doctor, Howard A. Rusk, who directed the largest rehabilitation center in New York. Having witnessed how far behind France was in this specialty, he invited me to work in his institute for a period of time.

In 1955 the Algerian War had not really started, despite the assassination there of two teachers in November 1954, and the flight nurses were not yet involved. Nonetheless, the fate of the veterans from Dien Bien Phu, those who were paraplegic or amputees, continued to concern me. This invitation seemed providential, and I decided to accept it and not to renew my contract.

A grant from the Atlantic Association allowed me to leave for the United States. My visit turned out to be a very rich professional experience. I was particularly impressed by the way the work was done in teams in the rehabilitation center. Every Monday we all came together—doctors, specialists, physical therapists, psychologists, and nurses—and studied the patients case by case, with an aim to effect a holistic rehabilitation, taking into account the psychological as well as the physical.

One evening I was invited to dinner at the Plaza Hotel by Gilbert Becaud, on tour in the United States. Since his Parisian fans had torn up the seats at the Olympia with unbridled enthusiasm for his show, his celebrity had crossed the Atlantic. Learning of my presence at Doctor Rusk's institute, he offered to come and sing before the young and not so young in training. "Mr. 100,000 Volts" lived up to his name. His talent was paired with immense kindness, and it was for me, and all the patients at the institute, an unforgettable evening. Before the enchanted eyes of the men in their wheelchairs, he sang many of the songs he had made famous in France. He was generous enough to repeat his performance after my return to Paris, when I worked at the Invalides rehabilitation center.

At the end of my training period in New York, a trip of studies in different centers of reeducation brought me to San Francisco. From there I went to Los Angeles, hoping to spend a week of vacation in Mexico, but I had overlooked an important detail: a visa. The writer Romain Gary, consul of France in that city, came to my rescue and welcomed me in his magnificent residence in Beverly Hills, immersing me for a few hours in that very special world of movie stars to which his wife, Jean Seberg, belonged.

On coming home to Paris I wanted to practice my newly acquired expertise by working at the center of reeducation at the Invalides. It was also at this time that Captain Jean de Heaulme and I married. I had met this young officer in Indochina in 1953. His father lived in Hanoi and we had common relatives, so I decided to visit him. He invited me to dinner with his son, who was then attached to the GCMA and based in Hanoi.

In 1954 Jean de Heaulme had been parachuted in the backcountry beyond Dien Bien Phu to lead an action of harassment against the Vietminh supply lines. Back in Hanoi after the fall of the camp, he had been attached to the staff of General Cogny to negotiate the liberation of the wounded and their return. Thus it was that on the day of my liberation, May 24, 1954, he was the third person to greet me, after General Cogny and General Dechaux. During the following days, he accompanied me to Lanessan Hospital as I visited the injured, since he needed to gather information for the negotiations.

That would have been as far as things went if circumstances had not brought us in touch again in Paris. I had no preconceived idea about the career of the man who was to become my husband, but I hoped that it would be one that would serve others, such as officer or doctor. Like many women, I believe, I need to admire before I can love. It seemed to me difficult to believe that Jean de Heaulme could have embraced his military life without courage, generosity, devotion, or an ability to give of himself. These were qualities that seemed to me indispensable for love to be more than a straw fire, something that would last through the joys and the challenges that are part of life. Looking back I admit that having married a military officer allowed me to share everything with him, my past in the air force and his vocation as a Marine officer and a paratrooper. For him this fidelity to the past, which meant so much to me, was natural; we have always been able to share harmoniously memories and projects for the future.

Our wedding took place on June 14, 1956, in the Church of the Invalides. The wounded who were at the center for rehabilitation were able to attend in their wheelchairs. Dien Bien Phu was still alive in everyone's mind, and the attendants had trouble fitting in the nave. Chance had it that one of my cousins was seated next to the mother of Lieutenant Rondeau, whom I had nursed over there and who had died since. She had difficulty pushing her way through the crowd, repeating, "I have the right to be here; she took care of my son!"

As we came out of the church, dozens of reporters crowded around us. The papers had announced our wedding, and the number of people present was amazing. The curiosity of some did not eclipse the warmth and the affection that emanated from them all.

After this new beginning I obtained the contract I had hoped for with the reeducation center of the Invalides. There I found again several men I had nursed in Dien Bien Phu. Defline, already fitted with a prosthesis, would come in from time to time. Heinrich Haas, a triple amputee, walked remarkably well with his false leg. The prostheses on his arms caused more problems, but as in Val-de-Grâce, he kept his extraordinary morale and lifted that of his comrades, less severely injured than he but far more depressed.

There I also found Bernard Hay, sergeant in the 8th BPC. In April 1954 shrapnel had severely injured his spinal cord, rendering him tetraplegic. His courage and energy were remarkable, and those traits of character never failed. After an operation and a long reeducation, he had regained partial use of his legs. Later, as he needed to have regular dialysis treatments, he had the idea, with his wife, a nurse, to create a dialysis center near Lourdes. He built it in five years, sparing pilgrims to Lourdes who were on dialysis the long drive to the larger neighboring cities. I saw him again in 1994. Because of arterial disease his legs had been amputated, one after the other, but his courage remained impressive. He was well supported by his wife, who directed the center with devotion and competence. This difficult and outstanding project probably enlivened and supported him until his last days.

Often at the Invalides, with a young paraplegic whose face I can still see though I have forgotten his name, I walked the long corridors and the stairs that he managed with the sole help of his arms and of his crutches. We sought to build in these young men the greatest possible independence. Moral strength and will were obviously necessary to their rehabilitation.

In 1959 my husband was assigned to Madagascar. Our oldest son, François, was three months old. For half a year I was only a wife and a mother, particularly since during the hot season our baby had difficulty adapting to the climate and was gaining practically no weight.

That was shortly after the Malgache independence, as Madagascar had become an autonomous republic in the French community and had gained its full independence in 1960. My husband was counselor to the chief of the Fianarantsoa province for problems of security and defense. He traveled much of the time, but our son was too young for me to accompany him. In this false "good climate" on the high plateau, cases of infant mortality were not rare; I saw a young French baby die of dysentery in a matter of a few hours. After the joys we knew the anxieties of parents, which were increased for me because of my isolation. We were housed apart from the other military cadres, and besides, many young women hesitated to approach me, intimidated by all the publicity about me still present in their minds. A real feeling of solitude was added to my worry over the health of our baby.

Luckily, once the hot season ended, everything fell into place. François became again a healthy, happy baby. I regained the freedom of mind that allowed me to volunteer again. I helped the social work association that had organized training in hygiene and child raising for the Madagascar military wives. I also went to the hospital at Fianarantsoa, following the visit of the military surgeon, to take charge of the rehabilitation he ordered with the limited equipment available. Madagascar had suffered a terrible polio epidemic, and many other patients there had been injured by cow horns. Distances were great, and only rarely could the wounded benefit from a sound physiotherapy. But what joy radiated from the unfortunates when they could recover a certain autonomy and leave us, even with their rustic crutches. I deeply shared this joy, and I had the feeling of still being useful.

Despite my need for connection and my desire for access and activity directed to others, I always gave priority to my family, especially when two more children, Véronique and Christophe, arrived to enrich our home. My husband's career allowed me to maintain my relationships within the military milieu. I met again many old friends from my Indochina years who knew me or my husband. Jean had spent his youth in Indochina and had there passed the entrance exam to St. Cyr, the French West Point. He had been a prisoner of the Japanese in 1945 and had served three combat tours during the Indochina War.

From its initiation in 1967, I had been a member of the National Association of the Veterans of Dien Bien Phu, based in Pau. It was impossible that so much solidarity shown by the men in combat should disappear without continuation, particularly when, in the silence of years, they were the only ones to preserve the living memory and the solidarity needed to support their comrades who had fallen in desperate conditions. I have always done all I could to attend their commemorations.

I was in the court of the Invalides, along with several veterans from Dien Bien Phu, on one day in June 1980 when the "unknown soldier" of Indochina was returned to France. The ceremony surrounding his return was presided over by Valéry Giscard d'Estaing, president of the French Republic. When it was over he came toward me and spoke words of praise. Not long after, I was nominated to the rank of Officer of the Legion of Honor. He decorated me on Place de l'Étoile on November 1, 1980, a radiant day when flag bearers from all over France formed a sumptuous crown around the Arc de Triomphe.

For the fortieth anniversary of Dien Bien Phu, celebrated in Pau in 1994, the minister of defense, François Leotard, pronounced a special homage to the combatants, as he had already done when he placed the first stone of their necropolis in Frejus. He then evoked a moment of profound emotion, saying, "The day Dien Bien Phu fell, I was thirteen, and I cried."

I maintained contact with the air force, where I found the team spirit that was unique for me. Every time I could, I came to visit Guite de Guyencourt, our chief flight nurse in Indochina, who brought together the old-timers. It was while my husband commanded the 2nd Regiment of Marines in Le Mans that I spent the most time with the families, supporting them in their isolation when their husbands left on mission for several weeks.

Our fidelity to our Indochinese past had for us a face and a name: Kun. A few months after we left Le Mans for Luneville, the drama in Cambodia occurred, with the fall of Phnom Penh in April 1975 and the subsequent genocide perpetrated by the Khmer Rouge. In France, Catholic Relief sent out an SOS. A certain number of Cambodian families had sent their sons abroad to save them from the Communist danger and to allow them to pursue their studies, as the lycée in Phnom Penh had already been bombed and closed. These were young people aged fifteen to seventeen, sent by their parents to host families in exchange for payment, but the hosts did not have the means to keep them after the total isolation of Cambodia.

Catholic Relief was seeking families who could take charge of these lost children, as well as others who could welcome them during summer vacation. I had followed with concern the dramatic events that were taking place in this country neighboring Vietnam and I kept remembering the incredible beauty at Angkor. I could not ignore this call for help. I was told of the arrival in August 1975 of a sixteen-year-old Cambodian boy. We welcomed Kun as well as we could, but it was very hard for him to arrive in a foreign country, alone and without news of his family, just when many witnesses were telling the world about the atrocities committed by the Khmer Rouge.

In September 1978, after Kun left us after a month of vacation, I received a letter from him: "I have found joy again, the true joy I had lost." The Red Cross had just informed him that his mother and his five brothers and sisters were refugees in Ho Chi Minh City. It took over three years of demands, formalities, and waiting before we would see them arrive in Paris—emaciated, tired, and silent, but free and so happy to be reunited.

Kun learned then the extent of the pain endured by his family: His father had been taken with the men who disappeared; his mother and his youngest sisters had been interned in a refugee camp, even though their visa for France had been granted; then they escaped, hiding during the day and walking at night to reach Ho Chi Minh City, where they lived in hiding until they left for France. That day, in a great movement of friendship and solidarity, more than one hundred people accompanied that family to the airport to protect them from a new arrest.

The ties that grew between Kun and ourselves, particularly between him and our oldest son, François, almost his twin, are still strong. He was a witness at our son's wedding, and we entertain him often. He is even closer now after asking my husband to be his godfather. He calls me "godmother" even though his real godmother is the remarkable person who took him and gave him the stability that, as a military family, we could not.

In 1981 the French government's move to the Left was for me a personal shock. I retained from the fight against the Vietminh a visceral antitotalitarian passion, and the presence of Communists in the government pushed me to engage politically. Still I refused to adhere to a party when I decided to engage in municipal action, which for me represented service and not personal ambition. It also was a way to remain accessible to everyone. This engagement was really a means to remain faithful to the past without locking myself into it. I presented myself in the municipal elections in 1983, which marked the start of eighteen years of service to the residents of my district.

After my election to the office of town counselor of my district, the mayor asked me to work in the domain of associations, which are the lifeblood of a district. During a meeting the APEI, an association for the parents of handicapped children, had asked the district council to devote more energy to the problems of the young mentally handicapped. With my background as a nurse and my contacts with the suffering, I asked the mayor if he would name me as a delegate to the handicapped. I then had the comforting feeling that I was closing a circle.

In close touch with the young parents and their teachers, I was able to take several steps toward the integration of handicapped children into schools. Those were very rich years, and although I had other responsibilities, such as being the representative of the mayor to three schools and working for social issues, it was that achievement that stood out for me from those eighteen years in city hall. I remain full of admiration for those parents who put so much love and imagination into their struggle to offer their children the maximum opportunities.

As a delegate to the Veterans Association, I maintained numerous contacts with all the associations united in a liaison committee, whose activities had as their object the duty of giving witness to the past. While I was involved in the veterans of the 17th Arrondissement, I could not forget those of Dien Bien Phu. Thanks to the immense devotion of their president, I could follow their cases: illnesses, hospitalizations, and deaths. One veteran in particular occupied a lot of my time. This was Corporal Tran The Ty, who had joined the French army as a volunteer in April 1953 then transferred to a Vietnamese battalion of paratroopers. I had nursed him in Dien Bien Phu, where, severely wounded in late March 1954, he had both legs amputated. Liberated by the Vietminh as an invalid, he was one of the indigent wounded that I had gone to see in a camp in Saigon with Doctor Grauwin in 1955. After the French left, he had been reduced to begging for his living.

Thanks to a benevolent group of veteran paratroopers, and with the assistance of the Ministries of Veterans and of Foreign Affairs, Tran The Ty had been repatriated to France with his family. He lived there on social security, in difficult and humiliating conditions because, considered a member of a foreign army, he could not aspire to a disability pension. On the advice of General Schmitt, who had fought in Dien Bien

Phu and was now governor of the Invalides, I wrote to the president of France. Jacques Chirac, moved by this tragic case, ordered that the dossier be reopened. This took several months. Luckily Tran The Ty was being supported by the paratroopers' association and that of the military handicapped in Toulouse. Administratively there was no solution. But Tran The Ty, having acquired French citizenship, presented a unique case as a double amputee. As an exception the minister of veteran affairs decided to grant him a disability pension.

I will always see him in my mind as he looked one day when he came to visit me in Paris without his prostheses, which hurt him, framed in the door of my apartment, perched on the shoulders of his son-in-law.

During my first two municipal tenures, Jacques Chirac was the unanimously elected mayor of Paris; he had accomplished the "union" that won him two grand slams at the municipal elections. On my third tenure, the Right tore itself apart, and this shocked me deeply. Then my tenure ended. Summer brought me back to the region where my father had been born and where we had renovated an old farm, Esbats. This helped me pass this change of life. This house had already allowed our children, too often forced to change schools by my husband's career, to find roots. It also was the place where later we received our three grandchildren, Arnaud, Alexander, and Ines. I believe they are already sensitive to the beauty of this part of France and that there they too will find those roots that are ours. It is another form of fidelity, one that we share with our children, and one that my cousin, Jean de Galard, has maintained in Saint-André as its mayor for the last forty-four years.

The life that is mine after Dien Bien Phu does not, of course, have the same exceptional character of those fifty-eight days, but I have tried to live it without ever betraying that past.

For a long time I nourished an old dream: returning to Vietnam. But I worried about being unable to travel incognito and I did not want to endorse the Marxist regime there, given the lack of freedom that still reigns in that country. A gradual opening of the regime and my new freedom from work finally allowed me to consider the possibility of a trip back to Indochina.

An opportunity came: A comrade of my husband was organizing a trip and the association Vietnam Hope wanted contacts in North Vietnam, where it as yet had no base. The association had been founded by an officer, a veteran of Dien Bien Phu, and a few fellow veterans who, after having lived in Indochina during so many years of peace and of war, wanted to lighten the misery of the neediest. Having witnessed the social assistance provided by the Christians, still among the most oppressed in Vietnam, they brought direct help to the bishops to support the reconstruction of holy sites, which would be the bases for community and assistance.

I wanted to revisit certain places and discover those where my husband's parents and grandparents had lived and where he himself had spent his youth. In fact, I wished to feel this country live, to sense anew its soul. My husband had no particular desire to return to Vietnam, as he preferred to maintain his memories intact, be they good or bad. But he decided to go for my sake and that of Vietnam Hope.

I did not want to revisit Dien Bien Phu. My memories were deep in my heart, and I chose to keep them there. I had seen a photo of the place, now a cement city of 20,000 inhabitants (80,000 if you included other residents of the valley), there where the bulldozers, digging the foundations of new houses, brought up the bones of the dead from that terrible battle. I could not have borne such depredation. In any case Dien Bien Phu was not on the itinerary of our trip, any more than Na San or Lai Chau, where I would have so loved to return.

Our voyage took us toward Cao Bang. Through witnesses of the past, fellow travelers, we relived the drama of Route C4 in 1950 in these abrupt mountain peaks overgrown with jungles and ideal for ambush. We went by That Khe, where Lieutenant de Fontanges had managed to evacuate the wounded released by the Vietminh. Then we continued toward Langson and the Bay of Along, in its frequent and fantastic aspect under mist and drizzle.

In Hanoi I found again the charm of Petit Lac, with its trees reflected in the water and its paths where smiling lovers walked arm in arm. Vitality and smiles did not reveal the burden of a totalitarian regime, yet a few tight faces, such as that of the woman at the post office, gave me the impression of another reality, more tragic, to which we had no access.

I searched in vain for the flight nurses' villa near Lanessan Hospital, also made unrecognizable by its Russian reconstruction. I would have wanted to see it again, full of memories as it was, particularly of that day when, barely back from Nha Trang, I left again for my first night landing to retrieve nineteen injured men, and that night when they told us that the plane on which our fellow nurse, Aimée Calvel, was flying had been hit and that she would not be coming back to Hanoi.

Our tour was leaving for Cambodia, but we decided to go up to Tonkin, in a pilgrimage to the places where my husband had spent his youth. Where his grandparents had worked, we met the ancient parish priest, ninety-three years old, who remembered them well. A beautiful new church under construction replaced the old one, which had been transformed into a catechism school. We realized the vitality of the Vietnamese people's Catholic faith.

My husband had expressed his desire to go to Keso to visit the first cathedral built in Tonkin, later dethroned by the construction of the one in Hanoi. We had been driving for a long time and the day had been tiring, particularly for the chauffeur. But when we announced that we were abandoning our project, it was the driver who said, "It is for God, let's go there!"

The next day our emotions were even stronger. Where my father-in-law had managed for fourteen years a concession of six thousand acres, of which eight hundred acres were planted in coffee trees, with 2,500 head of cattle for the manure, we ran into an old villager who evoked childhood memories with my husband. But mostly he sang the praises of "Monsieur de Heaulme," who "had done much to develop the country by introducing new crops, building a bridge," and so on.

I was profoundly moved and happy. I had proof of the attachment that many French had for this country, the country they had worked to develop and enrich for its own sake, and it explained the welcome that French tourists received almost everywhere in Vietnam. Already, in Nha Trang, the bishop had told us that thanks to Doctor Alexander Yersin, considered a benefactor of Vietnam, the province lived in a climate of freedom never found elsewhere. Yersin (1863–1943) was a microbiologist and military doctor of Swiss origin who discovered the plague bacillus and perfected an antiplague serum.

Our connection to Vietnam Hope led us to meet several bishops and religious orders. The Catholic Church is a strong force not only in the domain of the faith but also in the social realm, since social security does not exist in Vietnam. The nuns direct the clinics and the assistance to the poor and to the lepers, these poorest of the poor. They also run most of the nursing school classes. Since the fall of 2001, there has been some liberalization in the country. The nuns, who could only apply the children to manual labor, are now authorized to teach them the rudiments of reading, writing, and arithmetic during their last year in preschool. Thus without giving up its control over education, the Vietnamese government can reduce the number of illiterates.

In 1953–54, too occupied with my missions as a flight nurse, I had had no real contacts with the people of Vietnam. Those were limited to our chats with our *thi ba* (our maid at the villa) and with our Vietnamese patients. But the language was a real obstacle. This time, thanks to the efforts of my husband to refresh his Vietnamese and to our young interpreter, I had a feeling of knowing better these courageous people who smile even through hard times, and of understanding something of their souls: the deep patriotism of a people who have suffered so much throughout their history and manifest their attachment to the land; who, impassioned for freedom, feel a strong solidarity; and who want to show to all the nations a personality, a civilization of their own.

Everywhere, despite an apparent liberalization, the Marxist state, attached to its theories and its power, fears philosophies and religions that might undermine its base. It maintains control on the individual and on the economy, which restrains the development of the country and keeps a large part of the population in a state of great poverty. These constraints, sadly, totally deprive the ethnic minorities, still numerous on the plateaus and in the mountains, of their freedom.

Everything that touches Vietnam remains dear to our hearts, and my husband and I are happy to participate in the work of two associations that, without any political motive, labor in favor of the weakest: one being Vietnam Hope, with its religious perspective, the other being Hot Lua, the Grain of Rice, with its humanitarian purpose. These associations are particularly generous and unselfish, but they are not the only ones. Is not the world full of great people who are not talked about but who contribute to make it better?

Chapter Thirteen
TO THEM

My memoirs are at an end. They began "before" and continued "after" Dien Bien Phu. But it is the weeks lived over there among the wounded and the combatants that forever marked and changed my life.

Never at any time did I regret finding myself trapped in Dien Bien Phu. The difficult but exalting moments that I experienced there remain for me unforgettable, and I attach a great price to the friendship and the esteem of those brave men with whom I had the privilege to share my life for almost two months. So it is in thinking of all those who fought, of all the dead, of all the missing in action, of all those who will never be spoken of, and of their families, that I wrote this testimony. For weeks I dove back into that hell, unable to sleep again after waking up at night. And if I could not speak of every one of them, I hope they know that I do not forget a single one.

The questions often come up: Why Dien Bien Phu? How was there so much courage? In the face of such horror, how can one explain such ardor, tenacity, heroism?

Dien Bien Phu has sometimes been compared to Verdun, but at Verdun the wounded could be evacuated, relief troops were assured, and the combatants were giving their blood for their own country. In Dien Bien Phu, twelve thousand miles from France, they were fighting for the defense of freedom. Their fight had no other objective than the defense of the free world, side by side with the Vietnamese who, in a fratricidal war, had rejected the Communist universe, the gulags, the terror. At least after General de Lattre de Tassigny took command, matters were clear:

We had the duty to defend our promises, our solidarities, and our honor. "The combatants of Dien Bien Phu were—in the words of Napoleon Bonaparte—'giants' in their courage, their audacity, their comradeship and their self denial," wrote another reporter on the battle, and I subscribe entirely to his judgment.

In Dien Bien Phu I was deeply touched that the combatants considered me "one of their own." I have remained very grateful to the way these veterans have maintained our friendship. On the other hand, when I am referred to as a "heroine," I get somewhat annoyed. And even more so when people seem to believe that I am an exception, in some way not "like everybody else."

During the times of war or calamity that the world has known since 1954, and often as I wrote this book, I recalled all those, combatants or civilians, who, plunged together into adversity, came together in solidarity and gave all of themselves in a spirit of service greater than they. In this they manifested the greatness of humankind.

The reactions of the free world since Dien Bien Phu have shown that the battle had great value as a symbol. That alone justifies and explains the heroism of our combatants. Those men had the modesty to say nothing of it, but I wanted to testify for them, for they belong to our history, a history that deserves to be known and taught.

APPENDIX A

Some Testimonies

LETTER FROM COLONEL LANGLAIS

Malestroit, October 22, 1954

Dear Geneviève, I would like to receive news from you. I was told that you are now assigned to an airline in Africa. I also had echoes of your return to France and of your trip to the United States. I don't need to tell you that all your friends and companions in arms know that you were the prey of journalists. We know too well your simplicity and your modesty. Nonetheless I feel that what you did in Dien Bien Phu is not well known enough. No one knows that you volunteered to get on that plane on March 28 because you had been unable to go out on mission the day before. Few women in the world could have done what you did and I leap with furor when I hear the envious, especially the women, say that chance brought you to us and that anyone could have done the same thing. I would have liked to see those people in "the catacombs." They would have given us, like many men reputed to be courageous in Dien Bien Phu, a fine example of breakdown.

I know not if you have read the ridiculous book titled "Dien Bien Phu" that appeared May 18, which is considered semi official. I let its author know what I thought of this shameful commercial enterprise.

I also read in it the text of your citation altered by some indifferent interpreter. I will copy the text that I wrote one night in my post and demand through official channels that it be substituted for the other. [See the original citation below.] As to my *Dien Bien Phu*,

I burnt its pages before its end. It will never see the light of day. I tried but I cannot start again. I needed the ambiance of the battle, and my memories are already fading.

Good bye, dear Geneviève. Accept my amicable regards.

Langlais

PROPOSITION OF CITATION TO
THE ORDER OF THE ARMY
Mademoiselle Geneviève de Galard Terraube

Flight nurse of the G.M.M.T.A., only woman at Dien Bien Phu during the battle, stirred the imagination of all by her quiet courage and her smiling devotion.

Arriving on March 28 with the last medical plane able to land, she immediately placed herself at the disposal of the commanding doctor in the surgical unit.

On her own initiative, and despite the violent concentrations of enemy artillery, she visited every injured combatant in the center of resistance during the furious assaults from March 30 to April 2.

Living among the wounded, sleeping on a stretcher in the suffocating atmosphere of the unit, she lavished her attentions with untiring energy, at all hours of day or night.

With an unequalled professional competence and an indestructible morale, she was a precious assistant to the surgeons and helped save many lives.

She will always be, for the combatants of Dien Bien Phu, the pure incarnation of the heroic virtues of the French nurse.

For attribution,
Colonel Langlais, Defense Commander
p/o Captain Roy
April 1954

LETTER FROM MASTER SERGEANT
JEAN-BERNARD MONCHOTTE
February 25, 2002
Dearest Madame,

What a good idea that you are writing your memoirs!

I have known you well, particularly in the surgical unit and later over the course of our veteran reunions.

Like many of my combat comrades in arms of every rank, I had the good fortune in our trials to benefit from your unlimited devotion, from your generosity and your kindness. These are not just words. Many of the injured remained silent, but after these battles, the noise, the mud, I did not have occasion to tell you: we are all deeply grateful. The unit was always full. The less injured did not stay long but all of them have unforgettable memories of your presence, the care of a nurse in that inferno, a smile for each one; for the most grievously hit, it was their last memory.

You were full of attention to us, the small pieces of apple you handed out and the last cigarettes offered and as you responded to the moans that came from all around: "Madame, I hurt," "Madame, I have maggots," etc. I won't say more—

You must have been exhausted, wounded at your deepest core by so much pain and tragedy. You went on stubbornly and courageously with all your tasks, without losing your competence. There, Madame, is what I simply wanted to tell you, for forty years. Nothing is forgotten.

Madame, please accept my deepest respect.
Master Sergeant Jean-Bernard Monchotte
Veteran of the 8th Choc Battalion
Wounded April 5, 1954 at Dien Bien Phu

DIPLOMATIC TELEGRAM FROM HENRI BONNET, AMBASSADOR OF FRANCE IN WASHINGTON

The reasons for the exceptional success of this visit are multiple. The first is, without doubt, the emotion and admiration stirred in the entire country, by the battle of Dien Bien Phu, to which—as you well know—the press, the radio, and the television have given over the weeks such publicity that the memory of this unequal fight, symbol of the courage and vitality of the French people, is now firmly anchored in the American memory. France, on the other hand, continues to benefit in this country of numberless friends, happy to express themselves when the occasion arises. But these expressions of friendship would not have manifested themselves with such breadth and spontaneity if the personality of Miss de Galard had not immediately conquered the hearts of the public. She probably surprised everyone used to "glamour girls" eager for personal publicity. She charmed them all the more by her kindness, her simplicity, her authentic modesty, her common sense and the calm with which she responded to their questions. By never putting herself forward, by constantly reminding us of the heroism and sufferings of the soldiers in Dien Bien Phu, adding that it was they who should be remembered, she deeply impressed them. The commentators are many who quoted the phrase she never ceased repeating: "I only did my duty."

In short, her visit to the United States awoke feelings of sympathy and admiration, and the publicity given her responds perfectly to the intense desire of the American public for what is called here "human interest."

From the perspective of French public relations here in the United States, we can only congratulate ourselves for this trip that can be considered an exceptional success. Whatever the criticisms directed at France during these past weeks on the subject of Indochina, it is striking to note that the press, from the papers usually favorable to our country to the most isolationist, was unanimous in its homage to the "Angel of Dien Bien Phu," a homage that, through her, is addressed to the soldiers of the Expeditionary Corps and also to the French women and the young girls to whom the movies and a certain kind of literature too often give a deformed and unflattering image.

APPENDIX B

Order of Battle, French Union Forces, Dien Bien Phu

FTNV	Land Forces North Vietnam, Major General Cogny
GATAC	Tactical Air Group North, Brigadier General Dechaux
EDAP	Airborne Division Command Element, Brigadier General Gilles, replaced by
GOP	Operational Parachutist Group, Colonel Bastiani, replaced by
GONO	Operational Group Northwest, Colonel (later Brigadier General) de Castries
GM 6	Mobile Group 6, Lieutenant Colonel (later Colonel) Lalande
GM 9	Mobile Group 9, Lieutenant Colonel Gaucher, then Lieutenant Colonel Lemeunier
GAP 1	1st Airborne Group (Brigade), Lieutenant Colonel Fourcade
GAP 2	2nd Airborne Group (Brigade), Lieutenant Colonel (later Colonel) Langlais, then Major (later Lieutenant Colonel) de Seguin-Pazzis

AIRBORNE BATTALIONS (IN ORDER OF ARRIVAL)

6th BPC	6th Colonial Parachute Battalion, Major (later Lieutenant Colonel) Bigeard, then Captain (later Major) Thomas
2/1 RCP	2nd Battalion, 1st Parachute Light Infantry Regiment, Major Bréchignac
1st BPC	1st Colonial Parachute Battalion, Major Souquet
1st BEP	1st Foreign Legion Parachute Battalion, Major Guiraud

8th BPC	8th Parachute Shock Battalion, Captain (later Major) Tourret
5th BPVN	5th Vietnamese Parachute Battalion, Captain (later Major) Botella
2nd BEP	2nd Foreign Legion Parachute Battalion, Major Liesenfelt

INFANTRY BATTALIONS

1/13 DBLE	1st Battalion, 13th Foreign Legion Demi-Brigade, Major de Brinon, then Major Coutant
3/13 DBLE	3rd Battalion, 13th Foreign Legion Demi-Brigade, Major Pégot
3/3 REI	3rd Battalion, 3rd Foreign Legion Regiment, Lieutenant Colonel Lalande, then Major Grand d'Esnon
2/1 RTA	2nd Battalion, 1st Algerian Infantry Regiment, Captain Jeancenelle
3/3 RTA	3rd Battalion, 3rd Algerian Infantry Regiment, Captain Garandeau
5/7 RTA	5th Battalion, 7th Algerian Infantry Regiment, Major de Mecquenem
1/4 RTM	1st Battalion, 4th Moroccan Infantry Regiment, Major Nicolas
1/ 2 REI	1st Battalion, 2nd Foreign Legion Regiment, Captain (later Major) Clémonçon
2nd BT	2nd T'ai Battalion, Major Chenel
3rd BT	3rd T'ai Battalion, Major Thimonier
GMPT 1	1st T'ai Mobile Partisan Group, by company, various leaders

ARMORED CAVALRY

3rd EM/ 1st RCC	3rd Squadron (company), 1st Armored Cavalry Regiment, Captain Hervouët

ARTILLERY/MORTARS

2/4 RAC	2nd Battalion, 4th Colonial Artillery Regiment, Major Knecht
11/4/4 RAC	Battery 11, 4th Battalion, 4th Colonial Artillery Regiment

3/10 RAC	3rd Battalion, 10th Colonial Artillery Regiment, Major Alliou
GAACEO	Colonial Antiaircraft Artillery Group of the Far East (4 quad 50s)
1st CEMLP	1st Foreign Legion Parachute Heavy Mortar Company
1st and 2nd CMMLE	1st and 2nd Foreign Legion Composite Mortar Companies
GM/35 RALP	Marching Battalion, 35th Parachute Artillery Regiment
BAAL	Laotian Artillery Battery (soon withdrawn)

ENGINEERS

| 17 BGP | 17th Parachute Engineer Battalion |
| 31st BG | 31st Engineer Battalion (two companies) |

INTELLIGENCE

| 8th GC | 8th Commando Group, plus detachments |
| GCMA team | Mixed Airport Commando Group |

MEDICAL TEAMS

1st ACP	1st Airborne Surgical Team (withdrawn December 21)
3rd, 5th, and 6th ACP	3rd, 5th, and 6th Airborne Surgical Team
29th and 44th ACMs	29th and 44th Mobile Surgical Teams

COMMUNICATIONS

Three companies from various headquarters

AIR FORCE

195th DB	195th Airbase Detachment
1/22 GC	Fighter Group
21st and 23rd GAOA	21st and 23rd Aerial Artillery Observation Groups
21/374th Signal Company	21st Company, 374th Signal Battalion

Note: The above air units were stationed at Dien Bien Phu. Additional support (the vast bulk of the airpower) from Hanoi-area airports and naval carriers consisted of five fighter groups/flotillas, two bomber groups/flotillas, four transport groups, one reconnaissance squadron, one air liaison squadron, one helicopter evacuation unit, two French-sponsored civilian air transport units, and the contracted American Civil Air Transport (CAT) unit.

OTHER UNITS
Maintenance, supply, transportation, traffic and provost, and postal

TOTAL STRENGTH
Bernard Fall lists the total strength as of December 6, 1953 as 4,907; as of March 13, 1954, as 10,814; airborne reinforcements from March 13 to May 6 as 4,291; and the combined total as 15,105 plus 2,440 PIMs. Other sources put the total French Union troops at somewhat over 16,000. There were 1,161 known deserters; Colonel Langlais believed there were more than that. These numbers are misleading in terms of "effective combat troops" (infantry, armor, artillery) as of May 1, which numbered about 2,900 according to Langlais. Near the end, original assignments did not count for much. Most of the garrison—cooks, supply personnel, whatever—necessarily were riflemen.

Primary sources: Bergot, *170 Jours de Dien Bien Phu*; Fall, *Hell in a Very Small Place* (widely accepted as a seminal source); Nordell, *Undetected Enemy*; Roy, *Battle of Dien Bien Phu*; Simpson, *Dien Bien Phu*; Stone, *Dien Bien Phu*; Windrow, *The Last Valley.*

APPENDIX C

Casualties of French Forces at Dien Bien Phu

From November 20, 1953, to March 12, 1954

NATIONALITY	KILLED	MISSING	WOUNDED	TOTAL
French mainland	39	10	119	168
Foreign Legion	30	27	237	294
North African	28	10	190	228
Vietnamese	17	41	252	310
TOTAL	114	88	798	1,000

From March 13 to May 5, 1954

NATIONALITY	KILLED	MISSING	WOUNDED	TOTAL
French mainland	269	180	974	1,423
Foreign Legion	318	738	1,266	2,322
North African	191	433	983	1,607
African	15	1	53	69
Vietnamese				
French Union	261	156	955	1,372
ARVN	46	57	110	213
Auxiliary	42	41	95	178
TOTAL	1,142	1,606	4,436	7,184

From May 5 to May 8, 1954 (estimated)

ALL NATIONALITIES	KILLED	MISSING	WOUNDED	TOTAL
	900	Unknown	1,800	2,700

From November 20, 1953, to May 8, 1954

NATIONALITY	KILLED	MISSING	WOUNDED	TOTAL
French Air Force	15	94	6	115
French Naval Aviation	21	7	4	32
American CAT	2	0	1	3
TOTAL	38	101	11	150
GRAND TOTAL	2,194	1,795[1]	7,045	11,034[2]

Note: Hospital statistics (not including enemy treated or French Union troops treated on site and not admitted to a battalion or main hospital): 6,215 admissions, 739 operations, 324 evacuations, 252 deaths

PRISONERS TAKEN MAY 7–8, 1954

Eight hundred and fifty-eight of the most seriously wounded were later evacuated by French airlift, leaving about nine thousand[3] for death camp marches. During their four-month captivity, about half would die or simply disappear.

Primary source: Windrow, Martin. *The Last Valley* as compiled from:
  Fall, Bernard. *Hell in a Very Small Place* (widely accepted as a seminal source)
  Rocolle, Pierre. *Pourquoi Dien Bien Phu*
  Héduy, Philippe (ed.). *La Guerre d'Indochine 1945–54*

---

[1] Plus unknown, May 5–8
[2] Some sources give total as 13,050
[3] Some sources state as low as 6,500

APPENDIX D

Order of Battle, Vietminh Forces, Dien Bien Phu

People's Army of Vietnam—Vo Nguyen Giap, commander in chief
Dien Bien Phu Front—General Hoang Van Thai, chief of staff

304th Infantry Division, Colonel Hoang Sam
      9th Infantry Regiment
      57th Infantry Regiment
      345th Artillery Battalion
308th Infantry Division, Colonel Vuong Thua Vu
      36th Infantry Regiment
      88th Infantry Regiment
      102nd Infantry Regiment
312th Infantry Division,* Colonel Hoang Cam
      65th Infantry Regiment
      141st Infantry Regiment
      209th Infantry Regiment
      154th Artillery Battalion
316th Infantry Division, Colonel Le Quang Ba
      98th Infantry Regiment
      174th Infantry Regiment
      176th Infantry Regiment
      980th Artillery Battalion
      812th Heavy Weapons Company
351st Heavy Division (Reinforced), Colonel Vu Hien
      151st Engineer Regiment

237th Heavy Weapons Regiment
45th Artillery Regiment
675th Artillery Regiment
367th Anitaircraft Regiment
Field Rocket Unit
148th Infantry Regiment (independent, partial)

Note: Each division had about 10,000 men, and estimates of impressed or volunteer civilian labor forces to assist in constructing roads and in moving supplies vary, but 300,000 may be about right. Vietminh casualties—killed, wounded, and missing—will never be known accurately. General Giap said there were 30,000.

Primary sources: Fall, *Hell in a Very Small Place*; Roy, *Battle of Dien Bien Phu*; Simpson, *Dien Bien Phu*; and Windrow, *Last Valley*.

---

* This division would be "cloned" in the mid-1960s as 7th NVA Division, and in 1969 Colonel Haponski's task force would battle its 65th and 209th Regiments north of Saigon.

CHRONOLOGY A
French Indochina War, 1945–1956

1945

January	Charles de Gaulle continues from 1944 as leader of the Provisional Government of the French Republic
March 9	Japanese take control throughout Indochina in a coup and massacre or imprison many French military, civil servants, civilians
March 11	Titular emperor Bao Dai proclaims independence of Vietnam
July 26	Potsdam Conference accords, Vietnam above the sixteenth parallel to be occupied by the Chinese, below the sixteenth, by the British
August 6–25	Atom bombs, August 6 and 9; Japan announces surrender, Ho Chi Minh orders insurrection, and "August Revolution" begins, August 15; Admiral Thierry d'Argenlieu named high commissioner of Indochina, August 16; Bao Dai abdicates, announces new government under Ho, August 25
September 2	Japan formally surrenders; in Hanoi, Ho declares independent Provisional Government of Vietnam
September 11–12	British troops enter Saigon September 11, first detachment French troops arrive September 12
September 23–25	Under martial law, fighting in Saigon; General Vo Nguyen Giap states, "From that day began a war of national revolution"; Communist-led mob massacres 150 French men, women, children

October 5	Lieutenant General Philippe Leclerc arrives as commander in chief, Far East Expeditionary Forces, headquarters Saigon
October 25	First entirely French-led military operation, against My Tho in Mekong Delta

1946

January	Operation Gaur launched to control plateaus of southern Annam and liberate Nha Trang
January 9–12	Bloody anti-French riots erupt in Hanoi
January 20	Charles de Gaulle steps down as head of Provisional Government of the French Republic, succeeded by Felix Gouin
February 28	After clashes with Vietminh and Chinese in Tonkin, French and Chinese agree to plan for relief of Chinese forces by French forces in Tonkin
March 6	Accord signed between government of France and Ho, Vietnam to be in French Union; attempt to debark French forces at Haiphong met with Chinese fire
March 10	French debark unopposed at Haiphong
March 18	Leclerc marches into Hanoi at head of French troops
April 17	Dalat Conference opens to discuss form of government, ends in stalemate
May 5	French referendum rejects accord
May 11	Franco/Vietminh conference at Dalat ends in failure
June	Lieutenant General Jean Étienne Valluy succeeds Leclerc as commander in chief
June 1	D'Argenlieu proclaims the Republic of Cochinchina, the forerunner of successive "South Vietnamese" governments (GVN), with Nguyen Van Thinh its first president
June 10	Chinese complete withdrawal from Hanoi
June 19	Georges Bidault elected president of the Republic's Provisional Government
July–August	Conference at Fontainebleau to establish status of Vietnam ends in failure; however, modus vivendi

	is signed by Ho and French government on September 14, soon to be violated
November 11	Thinh commits suicide, feeling deserted by French, countrymen, friends
November 23	Incidents in Haiphong result in heavy fighting, including intense French artillery and air bombardment, with many Vietnamese civilian casualties
November 28	Vincent Auriol becomes president of the Republic's Provisional Government
December	Major General Georges Nyo named commander in South, with headquarters in Saigon; Le Van Hoach assumes presidency of Republic of Cochinchina
December 16	Léon Blum becomes prime minister
December 19	Insurrection in Hanoi; war in Indochina becomes widespread

1947

January–December	Valluy continues as commander in chief, Nyo as commander in South
January 16	Vincent Auriol elected president of Fourth Republic, continues to 1954
January 22	Paul Ramadier becomes prime minister
February	French garrisons in Tonkin are withdrawn to Hanoi
March 5	Émile Bollaert succeeds d'Argenlieu as high commissioner
March 11	French retake Nam Dinh
March 29	Reinforcements from France, intended for Indochina, diverted to Madagascar to quell insurrection
May	Major General Raoul Salan named commander in North (Tonkin); in South, watchtowers established along main supply routes with nearby garrison for reaction force
May 5	Ramadier government dismisses communist cabinet ministers
October 1	General Nguyen Van Xuan succeeds Hoach as president of Republic of Cochinchina
October 7–25	Operation Lea launched in Bac Kan, Thai Nguyen, Lang Son, Cao Bang area of Tonkin, and north and northeast of Hanoi, successful

November 19	Operation Ceinture launched south of Bac Kan and north of Hanoi, continues to December 20, modestly successful
November 24	Robert Schuman becomes prime minister, succeeding Ramadier
December 23	Cambodia and Laos enter French Union

1948

January–July	French control in Red River Delta of Tonkin is extended
February	Valluy recalled to France, Salan becomes commander in chief until Lieutenant General Roger Blaizot assumes command in April; Major General Boyer de la Tour succeeds Nyo as commander in the South
March 1	Saigon-Dalat convoy ambushed
May 20	In Saigon General Xuan forms first government of GVN in opposition to Ho Chi Minh's proclaimed government
June 5	Bao Dai and French high commissioner sign accord recognizing an independent Vietnam and its membership in the Associated States of the French Union
July 16	André Marie becomes prime minister, succeeding Schuman
August	Major General Charles Chanson succeeds Salan as commander in the North
September 5	Schuman again becomes prime minister, succeeding Marie
September 11	Henri Queuille becomes prime minister, succeeding Schuman
October 20	Léon Pignon succeeds Bollaert as high commissioner

1949

Pignon continues as high commissioner

| January 22 | Chinese Communists under Mao Tse-tung triumphantly enter Peking |
| March 8 | Emperor Bao Dai and President Auriol sign accord |

	recognizing independent Vietnam within French Union; beginning of Vietnamese National Army
June	Mission of General Revers to Indochina; report leaked to public causes scandal
July 19	Independent Laos accepted into French Union
September	Lieutenant General Marcel Carpentier succeeds Blaizot as commander in chief; Major General Marcel Alessandri succeeds Chanson in the North; Chanson succeeds de la Tour in the South; Catholic provinces of Bui Chu and Phat Diem in Tonkin rally to French
October 1	Mao proclaims People's Republic of China
October	General Vo Nguyen Giap launches "The Law," a major campaign in Tonkin
October 28	Georges Bidault becomes prime minister, succeeding Queuille
November 8	Independent Cambodia accepted into French Union
December	Chinese Communist troops arrive along Tonkin-China border

1950

January	Bao Dai cedes post of prime minister (GVN) to Nguyen Phan Long; recognition of Democratic Republic of Vietnam under President Ho Chi Minh by China, USSR; beginning of major influx of Soviet, Eastern Bloc, and Chinese military and economic aid to DRV; recognition of Associated States of the French Union by United States and Great Britain
January 20	Ratification of accords of Associated States: Vietnam, Cambodia, Laos
May 6	Tran Van Huu succeeds Long as prime minister (GVN)
June 25	Start of Korean War
July 2	Queuille becomes prime minister, succeeding Bidault
July 12	René Plevin becomes prime minister, succeeding Queuille
August 23	French government decides to send a battalion to

	support UN forces in Korea, attached to U.S. 2nd Infantry Division
September 18	Dong Khe falls to Vietminh
October 3–11	Major Vietminh offensive in Tonkin and Cochinchina; evacuation of Cao Bang and disaster of Le Page, Charton columns on RC4; French forced to evacuate That Khe, followed by Lang Son in Tonkin, and
November 2	Lai Chau and Lao Kay, and
December 8–12	Din Lap and all the border posts along the northern frontier of Tonkin
December 17	General Jean de Lattre arrives in Saigon and succeeds Pignon as high commissioner and Carpentier as commander in chief; Lieutenant General Salon as his second in command

1951

"L'Année de Lattre," the Year of de Lattre. De Lattre continues as high commissioner, Salan as deputy; Major General Gonzales de Linarès takes command in North; "de Lattre Line" of fortifications established around Hanoi-Haiphong; Major General Charles Chanson commands in South

January 13–17	Vietminh offensive in vicinity Vinh Yen repulsed
March	Battle of Mao Khe, Vietminh repulsed
March 3	Tran Van Huu becomes prime minister of GVN, succeeding Long
March 10	Queuille becomes prime minister, succeeding Pleven
April 19	Combined French/Vietnamese army Operation Méduse in Delta
May 29–June	Battle of Day, Vietminh repulsed
July 15	Bao Dai orders full mobilization, largely ineffective
August 11	Pleven becomes prime minister, succeeding Queuille
September	Major General Paul-Louis Bondis succeeds the assassinated Chanson
September 17	De Lattre goes to Washington to appeal for more U.S. aid, is well received
October 2–6	Vietminh attack Nghia Lo in T'ai High Region, repulsed
November 10–14	French retake Hoa Binh

1952

January	Linarès continues in North, Bondis in South as commander; de Lattre dies of cancer; Salan appointed interim high commissioner and commander in chief, confirmed in May
January 20	Edgar Faure becomes prime minister, succeeding Pleven
January–February	Heavy Vietminh attacks along Route 6 and in Delta
February 22	Operation Amarante, Hoa Binh evacuated
March 20	General Nguyen Van Hinh becomes head of the Army of Vietnam
March 8	Antoine Pinay becomes prime minister, succeeding Faure
April 1	Jean Letourneau succeeds Salan as high commissioner
June	Nguyen Van Tam becomes prime minister (GVN), succeeding Huu
June 3	In Cambodia, King Sihanouk personally assumes power
July–September	Operations Quadrille, Sauterelle, and Caïman in central Annam successful
September 4	UN refuses admission of Laos, Cambodia, and Vietnam
October	Vietminh offensive in T'ai High Region, Nghia Lo falls
November	French establish air-ground base at Na San in High Region; Operation Lorraine in Delta inconclusive
December 2–3	Vietminh repulsed at Na San

1953

January	Sweep Operations Normandie, Nice, Artois, and Bretagne in Red River Delta, mixed results
8 January	René Mayer becomes prime minister, succeeding Pinay
January 29	Annam, joint operations in Qui Nhon, An Khe vicinity, Central Highlands, with Vietnamese forces, largely disappointing results
March–April	Vietminh divisions invade Laos from northwest Tonkin; French post Sam Neua evacuated, Muong

	Khoua and Sop Nao fall; French fortify Plain of Jars and Luang Prabang in Laos
May	Lieutenant General Henri Navarre succeeds Salan as commander in chief; Major General René Cogny succeeds Linarès in North
June 3	French government recognizes independence of Associated States
June 27	Joseph Laniel becomes prime minister, succeeding Mayer
July 17	Operation Hirondelle raid on Lang Son in north-eastern Tonkin successful
July 27	End of Korean War; French Korea battalion moves to Vietnam
July 28	Operation Camargue northwest of Hue to clear RC1, "Street Without Joy," successful
August 7–12	Successful evacuation of air-ground base Na San
August 17	Maurice Dejean appointed commissioner general
September–October	Vietminh offensive in Laos; Lao-French mutual defense treaty, October 22
October–November	Operation Mouette in southern Delta, mixed results
November–March	Vietminh move divisions to High Region
November 20	Operation Castor launched: paradrop of three battalions to establish air-ground base at DBP
November–December	Vietminh surround DBP
December 7–12	Forced evacuation of Lai Chau north of DBP, heavy casualties
December 31	Combined action of Vietminh and Pathet Lao in central Laos; French withdraw from Tha Khet to Seno

1954

January–March	Operation Atlante in Central Highlands of Annam, mediocre results
January 12	Bao Dai appoints Prince Nguyen Phu Buu Loc as prime minister, succeeding Tam in GVN at Saigon
January 16	René Coty becomes president of French Republic, succeeding Auriol

January 25	Berlin Conference to set up Geneva Conference on Indochina and Korea
March 13	First Vietminh assault on DBP
April 7	President Eisenhower uses a term that, although used earlier by others, now becomes famous: "domino theory"
April 26	Geneva Conference opens
May 7	DBP falls
June 3	Lieutenant General Paul Ely appointed commissioner general and commander in chief, succeeding Dejean and Navarre
June 16	Bao Dai appoints Ngo Dinh Diem prime minister, succeeding Buu Loc; Bao Dai later moves to France
June 18	Pierre Mendès-France becomes prime minister, succeeding Laniel
June 24–30	In Annam evacuation of An Khe, GM 100 is virtually annihilated, including Korea battalion
July 20–21	Geneva Accords; Diem refuses to sign for South Vietnam, as does the United States
July 27	Cease-fire for Tonkin
Aug 1–7	Cease-fire for Annam, Cochinchina, Laos, and Cambodia
August	Beginning of exodus of Catholics to South Vietnam

FINAL STAGES, LATE 1954–LATE 1956

August 1954–56	French withdraw combat units, leave small advisory detachments in South Vietnam
1955	Diem declares a Republic of Vietnam in opposition to Ho's Democratic Republic of Vietnam
September 14, 1956	Eleven years and two days after first French unit from the exterior arrived in Saigon, the last French troops leave Vietnam

Note: This chronology was compiled from many sources; dates may vary slightly by source, partly because dates in the eastern time zone (Vietnam) sometimes were used, sometimes the western (France).

CHRONOLOGY B

Battle of Dien Bien Phu,
November 12, 1953–May 7, 1954

1953

November 12	Orders issued to establish a *base aéroterrestre* at Dien Bien Phu
November 15	Operation Pollux begins; evacuation of Lai Chau, fifty miles north of DBP
November 20	First day of Operation Castor; paradrop of three airborne battalions (6th BPC, 2/1 RCP, 1st BPC), their battlegroup headquarters (GAP 1), a company of engineers, and two batteries of artillery
November 21	Second day of Operation Castor; drop of two airborne battalions (1st BEP, 8th BPC), their group headquarters (GAP 2), division headquarters (EDAP), and a mortar company
November 22	Third day of Operation Castor; drop of one airborne battalion (5th BPVN); garrison numbers 4,560 troops; first aircraft lands, General Cogny visits; reconnaissance in force (RIF) into hills, continuing to November 24
November 23	Fourth day of Operation Castor; 1st T'ai Partisan Mobile Group (GMPT 1) marches into DBP; first bulldozer arrives by parachute
November 25	First C-47 Dakota lands; DBP airbase becomes operational with a control post (PCIA), code name Torri Rouge; two Vietminh divisions identified moving toward DBP

November 26	General Cogny visits
November 28	First T'ai partisan bands of GCMA infiltrate to DBP; Laotian artillery battery (BAAL) landed by Dakotas
November 29	General Cogny and General Navarre land to inspect, along with Major General Trapnell, USA MAAG; thereafter, until Vietminh assault on March 13, frequent visits by ranking French and American military and government leaders
Late November	3rd T'ai Infantry Battalion (3rd BT) arrives; observation aircraft and fighter bombers arrive, revetted at airfield
December 1–21	RIFs by companies and battalions to north, northeast, and northwest; heavy casualties incurred
December 2–10	Three airborne battalions lifted out of DBP to Red River Delta (1st BPC, 6th BPC, 2/1 RCP) to join strategic reserve
December 3–23	Operation Ardèche, French Union forces from Laos move toward Sop Nao in Laos to attempt linkup with Operation Regate forces moving from DBP, December 21–26; heavy casualties in Ardèche, little value
December 4	Béatrice occupied; 3/31 BG engineer company arrives
December 6	Giap broadcasts order of general mobilization
December 7	Colonel de Castries replaces Brigadier General Giles at DBP as commander, Operational Group Northwest (GONO) established at DBP; Colonel Piroth assumes command of artillery
December 7–22	Continued evacuation of Lai Chau, disaster
December 8	2nd T'ai Infantry Battalion (2nd BT) arrives
December 9	Cogny visits
December 11	Air force Brigadier General Dechaux visits
December 15–21	1st and 3rd Battalions of 13th Demi-Brigade Foreign Legion (1/13 and 3/13 DBLE), 3rd Battalion of 3rd Algerian Infantry Regiment (3/3 RTA), 1st Battalion of 4th Moroccan Infantry Regiment (1/4 RTM), 1st Battalion of 2nd Foreign Legion Regi-

	ment (1/2 REI), and Mobile Group 9 (GM 9) air-lifted in; remnants of GMPT 1, 1st T'ai Mobile Partisan Group, straggle in; Anne-Marie established
December 17	Navarre and Cogny visit
December 18	Ten stripped tanks start being flown in, then reassembled, all operational by January 17, forming 3rd EM/1st RCC, 3rd Squadron (company) of 1st Armored Cavalry Regiment
Late December	Remainder of 31st Engineer Battalion arrives, improves airstrip and defenses
December 24–25	Navarre and Cogny spend Christmas with troops
December 29–30	RIFs to north and south halted by Vietminh

1954

January 1–10	Groupe Mobile 6 (GM 6), 1st Battalion, 2nd Foreign Legion Regiment (1/2 REI) and 3rd Battalion, 3rd Foreign Legion Regiment (3/3 REI) arrive
January 3	General Navarre, Cogny, and High Commissioner Dejean visit
January 5	Giap arrives at headquarters site nine miles north of DBP to take personal command
January 6–12	RIFs to north and south, mixed results
January 25	Expected Vietminh attack does not materialize; 5th BPVN withdrawn from DBP
January 26	General Blanc, chairman Joint Chiefs of Staff, visits DBP with Navarre, Cogny, and Dejean
January 29	De Castries ordered to conduct strong reconnaissance in force missions beyond the perimeter; French attacks on Vietminh positions until mid-February; few lasting results
January 31	Vietminh heavily shell airstrip, Éliane, and Dominique; active antiaircraft fire
February 1	Map with most recent French positions lost to enemy
February 2	Visit by highest-ranking American, Lt. Gen. John O'Daniel, MAAG
February 6–7	GAP 2 forces RIF to east and southeast, take heavy casualties

February 9	Legion and T'ai units RIF from Huguette west, mixed results
February 10–14	GAP 2 RIF to north, mixed results
February 14	Visit by General Ely, new chairman Joint Chiefs of Staff
February 17	After assessing heavy losses, Cogny orders that henceforth RIFs be limited to light reconnaissances by commandos
February 18	Berlin Conference announces Geneva Conference for April 26
February 19	Visit by Minister of Defense Pleven and French air force chief of staff, General Pierre Fay
Late February	Fortress DBP takes virtually its final shape
March 2	Four quad 50s arrive, become crucial to defense
March 4–5	French attack to north incurs heavy losses, unsuccessful
March 6	Navarre and Cogny make last joint visit; Cogny repeats his order of only light reconnaissance
March 11	GAP 2 attacks enemy digging approach trenches just beyond Béatrice, unsuccessful; enemy artillery fire on airfield extremely heavy from now on
March 12	Cogny makes last visit, sees many burned-out aircraft lining landing strip, inspects Béatrice; his aircraft later takes off under artillery fire; American Civil Air Transport (CAT) crews begin C-119 drops over DBP
March 13	Vietminh assault opens at 5:00 PM with massive shelling; Béatrice falls just after midnight
March 14/15	5th BPVN returned to DBP by parachute, suffer significant casualties, but some units reach assigned positions; Gabrielle initially survives assault, falls 9:00 AM on March 15; Piroth, the artillery commander, commits suicide
March 16	Major Bigeard's 6th BPC, a surgical team, and others dropped to reinforce
March 17	Serious desertion of T'ai from 2nd BT, 3rd BT; last DBP observation plane destroyed; air force fuel and ammo dump exploded; another airborne

	surgical team successfully dropped; Anne-Marie 1 and 2 lost; Anne-Marie 3 and 4 become Huguette 6 and 7
March 18	Burial in cemetery is huge problem; De Castries orders that henceforth French KIAs be buried on the spot
March 19/20	Dominique 4 becomes Sparrowhawk; Claudine 6 becomes Juno (Junon)
March 21–26	Defensive fighting positions and trenches improved and minefields extended; both sides shuffle forces, resupply for further action; increased air strikes on Vietminh positions as approach trenches come closer to French lines; heavy Vietminh antiaircraft fire; Éliane reinforced
March 22	Bigeard's 6th BPC, supported by tanks, successfully opens road to Isabelle; artillery replacements parachute into Isabelle
March 22	Langlais assumes de facto operational control of garrison; Bigeard directs counterattack operations; de Castries maintains liaison with Hanoi
March 27	Last C-47 to take off from DBP
March 28	C-47 medevac lands in darkness with Geneviève de Galard aboard, hours later destroyed by artillery. Bigeard counterattacks to west with three paratroop/infantry battalions and a tank platoon to destroy antiaircraft positions, successful
March 29	Extremely heavy monsoon rains continue; Isabelle succeeds in evacuating some wounded to main position at DBP
March 30	At 6:00 PM massive Vietminh attack; beginning of Battle of the Five Hills—Dominique 1 and 2, Éliane 1, 2, 4—and attack on Huguette 7; French counterattack; heavy casualties both sides; Isabelle now permanently cut off from main position at DBP
March 31	Bigeard counterattacks Dominique and Éliane; attempt to break through to DBP from Isabelle fails; counterattack stalls and D2, D5, and E1 retaken by Vietminh

April 1	Small number of paratroops from 2/1 RCP successfully dropped; Vietminh attack Huguettes
April 2	Huguette 7 abandoned; another small number of 2/1 RCP dropped; Isabelle under heavy artillery fire
April 3	Huguette 6 under heavy attack, tank counterattack successful; large number of 2/1 RCP dropped
April 4	2/1 RCP occupies Éliane 10 and Dominique 3; Vietminh withdraw from Éliane 2
April 5–6	Battle for Huguette 6; Bigeard counterattacks successfully, casualties high both sides
April 6–9	Relative calm; units shuffled, resupplied both sides
April 7	Another serious desertion by T'ai soldiers
April 9–10	About half of 2nd BEP dropped to reinforce, remainder dropped by April 12
April 10–11	Bigeard attacks Éliane 1, takes it, sustains heavy casualties; Vietminh counterattack fails
April 12	Vietminh attack on Éliane 1 fails but causes heavy casualties
April 13	Heavy shelling of DBP headquarters and Claudine 6
April 14–17	Attempts to consolidate and stabilize positions costly in casualties to both sides; food depot destroyed, garrison goes on short rations, April 15; promotion of de Castries, Langlois, Lalande, Bigeard, and others, April 16; entire garrison awarded Croix de Guerre, April 17
April 18	Huguette 6 evacuated under pressure; northern one-third of airstrip under Vietminh control
April 19	Nonparachutist volunteers dropped, most landing behind enemy lines and lost
April 20	Isabelle completely out of food; launches successful tank-supported counterattack beyond strongpoint Wieme, which is later lost
April 21–22	Airborne replacements trickle in, continuing for next few days; Vietminh artillery destroys last of DBP's trucks; Operation Condor relief force from Laos making slow progress, ultimately fails
April 23	Huguette 1 falls, Bigeard counterattack fails, leaving no operational reserve; one-half of

	airstrip in Vietminh hands; stongpoint Opera evacuated to new unnamed strongpoint; heavy monsoon rains continue
April 24–25	Vietminh continue pressure; antiaircraft fire increases
April 26	Fifty aircraft struck, three shot down; Geneva Conference opens
April 27	2/1 RCP and 5th BPVN raid on Élianes successful
April 28	One stick of Foreign Legion paratroopers dropped on Isabelle
April 29	Mud in trenches now 3 feet deep; food and ammunition depots hit and explode; garrison goes on half rations; one tank remains operable
April 30	Foreign Legion Camerone Day celebrated with meager resources
May 1	May Day celebrated by Vietminh; red flags fly over their positions; enormous artillery shelling marks beginning of their final attack
May 2	Éliane 1, Dominique 3, and Huguette 5 fall; one company of 1st BPC parachutes into main position; Isabelle retakes Wieme
May 3	Enormous monsoon rains, flak
May 4	Headquarters and another company of 1st BPC parachute into DBP; counterattack on fallen Huguette 4 fails
May 5	More men of headquarters and a company of 1st BPC dropped; de Castries authorized by Cogny to attempt breakout
May 6	Except for one company, remainder of 1st BPC dropped as last reinforcements; C-119 of U.S. Civil Air Transport shot down, pilot "Earthquake McGoon" killed; early in day only remaining French-held positions are Huguette 2 and 3, Sparrowhawk, Dominique 4, nameless strongpoint at airstrip, Lily 1 and 2, Juno, parts of Élianes, all of Claudine 5, and Isabelle; at noon enemy fires Katyusha rockets for first time, exploding depots; after dark many positions overrun

May 7   Remaining positions continue to fall under massive
                         assault; de Castries orders cease fire as of 5:00 PM.
                         At 5:30 PM Vietminh walk into command bunker

Primary sources: Bergot, *170 Jours de Dien Bien Phu*; Fall, *Hell in a Very Small Place*; Roy,
Battle of Dien Bien Phu; Simpson, *Dien Bien Phu*; Stone, *Dien Bien Phu*; and Windrow,
Last Valley.

Suggested Reading

Bergot, Erwan. *Les 170 Jours de Dien Bien Phu*. Paris: Presses de la Cité, 1979. A professional soldier, Bergot commanded a mortar company of 1st BEP at DBP. Taken prisoner at the fall of DBP, he was one of the few who survived the hell of the prisoner of war camps.

Curry, Cecil B. *Victory at Any Cost: The Genius of Viet Nam's Gen. Vo Nguyen Giap*. Washington, D.C.: Potomac Books, 1997. An AUSA Book. Biography. Part 3 is on Dien Bien Phu.

Duiker, William J. *The Communist Road to Power in Vietnam*. 2nd ed. Boulder, Colo.: Westview Press, 1996. A political history, 1900–1975.

Fall, Bernard. *Hell in a Very Small Place: The Siege of Dien Bien Phu*. Philadelphia: J. B. Lippincott, 1967. A seminal study. Fall, a naturalized French citizen, journalist, and university professor in the United States, got much of his information firsthand by accompanying French and, later, American, troops. He was killed by a mine in Vietnam a few months after he completed this book.

Giap, Gen. Vo Nguyen. *Dien Bien Phu*. Hanoi: Foreign Languages Publishing House, 1984. Much of the book is on background, strategy, and theory; there is disappointingly little on tactics and battle events.

Giap, Gen. Vo Nguyen, and Gen. Van Tien Dung. *How We Won the War*. Philadelphia: RECON Publications, 1976. Guidance for revolutionary warfare.

Herring, George C. *America's Longest War: The United States and Vietnam, 1950–1970*. 2nd ed. New York: Alfred A Knopf, 1986. Chapter 1 is on American-French relations, 1950–54.

Ho, Chi Minh. *Ho Chi Minh on Revolution: Selected Writings*. Edited by Bernard B. Fall. New York: New American Library, 1968. Writings from 1920 to 1966.

Lawrence, Mark Atwood, and Fredrik Logevall, eds. *The First Vietnam War: Colonial Conflict and Cold War Crisis.* Cambridge: Harvard University Press, 2007. Essays by historians.

Nordell, John R., Jr. *The Undetected Enemy: French and American Miscalculations at Dien Bien Phu, 1953.* College Station: Texas A&M University Press, 1995. Liberal references to political and military documents.

Roy, Jules. *The Battle of Dien Bien Phu.* New York: Carroll & Graf, 2002. Written with passion by an Algerian-French colonel, a friend of Camus, who resigned in protest of policy in Indochina.

Simpson, Howard R. *Dien Bien Phu: The Epic Battle America Forgot.* Washington, D.C.: Potomac Books, 1994. An AUSA Book. As a U.S. Information Agency war correspondent, then diplomat in Indochina, Simpson extensively covered French operations. Landing on November 23, 1953, in one of the first C-47s to use the airstrip, he accompanied Bigeard's battalion in a RIF to the north. Years later he extensively interviewed General Giap. A compact, excellent history.

Spector, Ronald H. *Advice and Support: The Early Years of the U.S. Army in Vietnam, 1941–1960.* New York: Free Press, 1985. Traces the deepening, tragic involvement of the United States in Vietnam.

Stone, David. *Dien Bien Phu.* London: Brassey's, 2004. Excellent pictures and tables depicting forces and actions. A brief, authoritative account.

Thiébaud, Éric, and Jean-Vincent Bacquart, eds. *La Guerre d'Indochine (1945–1954).* Paris: Éditions Tallandier, 1999. Brief but excellent coverage of the entire war.

Windrow, Martin. *The Last Valley: Dien Bien Phu and the French Defeat in Vietnam.* Cambridge, Mass.: Da Capo Press, 2004. An extraordinary synthesis of secondary sources, with excellent photos, sketch maps, and appendices.

Index

About the Author

After her release by the Vietminh, **Geneviève de Galard** worked tirelessly for proper medical treatment of the prisoners, as well as their freedom. Adored by the world media for her courage, skills, and compassion, she turned down movie and book offers until finally, for the fiftieth anniversary of the fall of DBP, her veterans implored her to tell her story. The resulting book, in French, was awarded the Grand Prix de L'Académie des Sciences Morales et Politiques.

Soon after her return to Paris in 1954 she was invited to the United States by President Dwight Eisenhower. In New York she was honored with a ticker-tape parade up Broadway. In Washington, D.C., she received a standing ovation in Congress and received the Medal of Freedom at the White House from President Eisenhower.

Two years after the fall of DBP she married Jean de Heaulme, a French special services officer who had parachuted into the Hill Country north of DBP to rally Montagnard tribes against the Communist forces. Geneviève was an army wife during the remainder of his career, always working for the betterment of both French and Vietnamese veterans and their families. Later, she served for many years as a councilwoman in Paris with a focus on services for the disadvantaged and handicapped. She continues to be invited to speak at veterans' affairs in France and accepts as many invitations as she can. She was invited to speak in October 2010 at the Association of the United States Army Convention in Washington, D.C. and to meet with several groups, including nurses in our armed forces.